Good News For The Captives

Bible Lessons For
Jail/Prison Ministry

Nancy Holloway

Copyright © 2019 Nancy Holloway
All rights reserved.
The lessons in this book and the materials in the Appendix
can be photocopied to distribute to the participants.

ISBN: 9781087183664

Cover design by Audrey Wagner. Stock photo ID:1043441246

DEDICATION

This book is dedicated to the many women over the past 16 years who have moved through
the Fayette County Detention Center—with love and gratitude for our
shared fellowship on our journey to God.

Table of Contents

Acknowledgements i

Introduction 2

Prayer

Prayer: Talking To God, Listening To God 6

Dear God, Help Me To Persevere In Prayer 12

Dear God, Help Me To Pray The Psalms 17

Prayer: Doorway To God 22

Warfare In Prayer: Winning Battles God's Way 28

Suffering

How God Uses Our Sufferings 36

The Stop Signs In Our Lives 42

God, Help Me Get Out Of The Pit! 48

Dear God, Please Help Me Deal With The Missing Pieces In My Life 53

God, When The Storms Of Life Assail Me, Help Me To Trust In You 59

Comfort

Lord, When I Carry Heavy Burdens, I Need Your Comfort 66

Dear God, Send Your Peace Into My Troubled Heart 71

The Good Shepherd Goes After The Lost Sheep 77

God Is With Me In The Detours Of My Life 83

Dear God, Help Me To Replace My Fear With Faith In You 88

Guidance

Dear God, Give Me Strength For The Journey As I Struggle To Follow In Your Steps 94

Dear God, Help Me To Forgive In Order To Repair Damaged Relationships 99

Open To Me Your Healing Love As You Did For Women In The New Testament 105

Dear God, Help Me To Realize That You And I Are Co-Creators Of My Life 111

God, Help Me To Trust You In Times Of Doubt 117

Spiritual Growth

Waiting For God 123

Set Your Heart On The Greatest Gift, Which Is Love 129

Dear Christ, We Are Called To Be Like You 135

Dear God, Free Me From The Idolatry Of Addiction 142

Dear God, Fill My Empty Heart With The Fruits Of The Spirit 148

Appendix 153

About The Author 169

ACKNOWLEDGMENTS

I owe profound gratitude and appreciation to the following for assistance in the development and completion of this book. I thank Ellie Sutter for being the first to suggest that I formalize and publish my "jail lessons" and for editorial assistance and encouragement. I thank Hawley Stevens, who spent hours correcting the manuscript and providing editorial suggestions and who continued to insist, when my own energy was flagging, that this material should be published. I thank Audrey Wagner for her editing and formatting work, for her cover design, and for assistance with the publishing process. I thank Rebecca Wilson for technical assistance and continued encouragement and support. Finally, I thank the staff members of the Presbyterian Church U.S.A. for graciously allowing me to use the format for these lessons that they used in publication of their book, *Standing in the Need of Prayer: Devotions for Christians in Prison*.

INTRODUCTION

This is an excerpt from an article I wrote for the spring 2011 Orthodox Peace Fellowship journal IN COMMUNION a number of years ago. It gives information as to how I conducted the one-hour study session with women at the Fayette County Detention Center who I visited each week for 16 years. This might be helpful as you plan your use of the lessons in this book.

"Do the time, don't let the time do you" are words I hear from the women I visit each week at the local jail. The ones who come out for Bible study are the ones who have chosen to believe that this is the beginning of an experience that can have profound meaning in their lives. They are open to the possibility that God is trying to get to them, and they are willing to let go and let that happen. Some are more serious, committed, and farther along in the journey than others, but all would share in seeing, as one chaplain described it, that jail can be a "womb of transformation."

When I open the Bible study session every Monday, I begin by suggesting to the women that they see the cup half full rather than half empty, because even in jail, there surely are some good things in their lives. They share their statements of gratitude with the group. More often than not, a number of them will say, "I'm grateful for being here," "I thank God that he put me here," and "I'm thankful I'm away from the drug dealer" (or the abusive husband, the battles with family members, addictions, prostitution, etc.), the implication being that this is "time out" to enable them to begin to go in a different direction.

The lessons that I offer address several major themes presented in various ways using many different scriptural references. These themes include prayer, how much they are loved by God, forgiveness, deification, suffering as it relates to their life in Christ, and a strong emphasis on getting into a church when they leave. I give every woman I encounter an icon (picture) of Christ with a Scripture verse on the back, "Fear not, for I am with you." (Isa. 41:10)

The lessons always begin with a Psalm (I encourage them to read a Psalm every day). I include about 6-7 Scriptures relating to the theme, as well as several readings from either contemporary sources or church or desert fathers on the subject. The lesson begins with a prayer and ends with the group praying together, each voicing their special request to God in shared concern for each other. The strong emphasis on prayer involves telling them this is a great opportunity to grow in prayer, and those with separate cells (the high risk) can do as the desert fathers say: "Stay in your cell and your cell will teach you everything." I urge them to pray for each other, their families, the guards, the judges, their victims, their enemies.

As we close the session, I ask them to tell me one thing they want me to pray for, and I will pray for them each day when I pray for my own children. Some of their prayer requests include, "Pray that my little children will remember me when I get out," "I want to be given wisdom to see my role in life and what God wants me to do when I leave here" (this from a woman whose child was murdered), "Protect me from those negative influences in my life," "Ask God to protect and nourish me," "More than anything, I want to do God's will," and "Pray that I won't give birth to my baby in jail."

I sometime sense that I'm entering the real world out there, a world of real people who have hit bottom, who admit they have done wrong, who are facing it, owning it, willing and eager to grow, and hungry and thirsty for righteousness.

When I leave the jail and head home encountering the chimera all around me of myriad addictions, denial, false selves, rampant materialism, the unholy drive for total satiety of all this world offers, I sometime wonder, who are the real prisoners?

Everyone I know who has been in jail/prison ministry stresses the fact that they receive far more than they give. I certainly have experienced that in my many years of ministry to the women at the Fayette County Detention Center.

Other Suggestions

1) To encourage sharing, openness, and bonding among you and the inmates, it helps to share some of your life experiences with them. If you trust them with your story, they are more likely to trust you with theirs and thus open up to you and to fellow participants. This seems to be particularly beneficial as they share their experiences with each other. I've seen far more comfort and wise instruction from one inmate to another than any I can give them. This is simply because they have been where their sisters or brothers have been.
2) You will realize early on that much prayer leading to discernment should be a major part of your ministry to inmates. This will be an aid to developing humility, remembering that Hebrews says we should be with the prisoners as if we are one of them. We might be aware of the possibility that many of us have done more evil than they have done, they just happen to have been caught!
3) Sometimes if we are sensitive to the direction the conversation is going, it is good to set the lesson aside and listen. As mentioned in # 1 above, it is amazing to hear the wisdom which oftentimes comes from the mouths of the incarcerated.

Lesson Instructions

The first two pages of each chapter are the lesson, which can be photocopied and given to the participants. The Commentary & Discussion sections that follow the lessons are simply guidelines for the leader. Feel free to use your own observations and experiences to enhance the commentary. Also, add other questions that may provoke discussion and sharing.

In the Appendix are optional helps, and you may have others. Please feel free to copy any/all of those and any part of the commentary to give to the prisoners along with the lessons.

PRAYER

Prayer: Talking to God, Listening to God

God, when all I had left was You, I realized that You are all I need. I long to grow closer to You, especially during times of suffering, sadness and pain. I know these times of affliction can bring me closer to You and change me into your likeness, but only if I surrender totally into Your loving and compassionate arms. I know this can happen only through a life of prayer and staying close to Your Word. So, dear God, teach me to pray in a way so that I can become truly Your trusting, loving child. In the name of the Father, the Son and the Holy Spirit. Amen.

VOICES FROM THE BIBLE

Psalm 1-150. Every Psalm is a prayer, and every human emotion is found in the Psalms. What is your favorite?

1) Luke 19:1-10 — *Zacchaeus desired to see Jesus*
2) Luke 18:9-14 — *The publican faced his sins and repented*
3) Matt: 6:7-15 — *Forgiveness is essential to spiritual growth*
4) Matt. 6:5-6 — *Come apart and pray*
5) 1 Thess. 5:16-21 — *Pray without ceasing*
6) 1 Kings 19:9-12 — *A still small voice*

OTHER VOICES

A quiet place ... A ready heart... An open mind. These are the things that we need in order to have a true praying spirit. We do not need to wail and moan. We do not need to speak volumes of well-crafted words. We have only to present ourselves, broken as we are, and reach out to the Lord to fix us. There is, of course a time for community prayer and praise. There is a time to raise the roof with song. But all praise, all song, begins with the quiet kernel of thought and reflection. And that is what we need strive for as we deepen our personal life with the Lord.
-Maureen Platt

The truth of the matter is, we all come to prayer with a tangled mass of motives—altruistic and selfish, merciful and hateful, loving and bitter. Frankly, this side of eternity we will never unravel the good from the bad, the pure from the impure. But what I have come to see is that God is big enough to receive us with all our mixture. We do not have to be bright, or pure, or filled with faith, or anything. That is what grace means, and not only are we saved by grace, we live by it as well. And we pray by it.
-Richard Foster

More things are wrought by Prayer
Than this world dreams of.
Wherefore, let thy voice
Rise like a fountain for me night and day.
For what are men better than sheep or goats
That nourish a blind life within the brain,
If, knowing God, they lift not hands of prayer
Both for themselves and those who call them friend?
For so the whole round earth is every way
Bound by gold chains about the feet of God.
-Alfred Lord Tennyson

To seek God
Means first of all
To let yourself be found by Him.
He is the God of Abraham, Isaac and Jacob.
He is the God of Jesus Christ.
He is your God
Not because He is yours
But because you are His.
To choose God
Is to realize that you are known and loved
In a way surpassing anything you can imagine
Long before anyone had thought of you or spoken your name.
-Esther de Waal

YOUR VOICE

1) *Do you find it difficult to pray? What are some of the resources you use to help you to pray?*
2) *What type of activity interferes with your prayer life?*
3) *Paul says we should pray without ceasing. What does this mean?*
4) *How does praying with others help or hurt your own prayer life?*
5) *How can being silent/listening to God be helpful to you?*
6) *Have you tried Centering Prayer? Was it helpful?*

COMMENTARY & DISCUSSION

Prayer: Talking to God, Listening to God

Introduction

What is prayer?

It is developing a RELATIONSHIP with God, coming into communion with Him, seeing Him as the most important relationship in your life, before all others, family, friends, neighbors, etc. Other relationships cannot work if God is not first in our lives.

Of course, part of prayer is asking for help, for your needs to be met—physical and spiritual. Also, intercession for others, praise, and thanksgiving are all important parts of prayer, but the relationship is the most important.

God may allow/use suffering to get your attention, so that you will turn to Him and get to know Him. Why? Because developing that relationship with God is what is going to transform you into His likeness.

Most of us see prayer as our talking to God, but as you get to know Him you talk less and listen more. We'll talk about a way of listening to God at the end of this lesson.

1. Psalms 1:1-50

We are not going to read 150 Psalms! I put this first because the Psalms are the prayers of the Church and have been from the beginning. The Christian church carried this tradition over from the Jewish tradition because early Christians did not have a New Testament (canon established in 400 C.E.) so they used the Psalms as part of their worship and prayers in the early liturgies.

We should pray a Psalm every day because every emotion known to us is in the Psalms. There are Psalms of joy and praise. Some of them are 8, 16, 21, 66, 67 and 100. But there are also many songs of lament that express despair and anger, such as 3, 22, 44, 57, and 74. Whatever our emotional state may be, we can find a Psalm that will speak to that particular concern.

As we talk about prayer, I want to point out three requirements for prayer. There are others, but these are the most important.

2. Luke 19:1-10

What did Zacchaeus want more than anything? What did he do to achieve it?

He wanted to see Jesus so badly that he climbed a tree and risked being laughed at to see this famous Teacher. When the Lord saw how eager he was to see Him, He invited himself to Zacchaeus' house.

And Zacchaeus was so humbled at this love shown to him, he vowed, as a tax collector who had stolen from so many people, to return all he had taken from them.

We have to show such a desire to see Jesus, to get to know him and allow Him to come into our house. In Revelation, He says "I stand at the door and knock." We must be eager to open that door and let the Lord in.

The first condition for true prayer is to long for and have the desire to see spiritually and to get to know God.

3. Luke 18:9-14

Why was the publican more justified? The Pharisee had kept all the rules. Why was he not the one who impressed God the most?

Because God is not so much interested in our keeping all the rules, as He is in us recognizing our need for Him. And only when we recognize that need can we truly enter a relationship with Him and begin to be changed into His likeness.

Christ didn't come to make bad men good, He came to make dead men live. In other words, He didn't come just to help us keep a system of rules. He came to transform us, which will not happen unless we realize how needy we are for God and become humble enough ask Him to have mercy on us.

The Prodigal Son parable, the most beautiful of all Jesus' parables, makes this clear. Only when the son was reduced to eating in the pig sty and realized he was "dead" did he know his only hope was to return to his father for forgiveness and complete restoration, which his father offered him in full.

We don't need a little fixing up; we need transformation, and we have to recognize that we need it before it will begin to happen.

The Greek word for repentance—*metanoia*—doesn't mean just cleaning up your act a little; it means turning around, changing direction, heading toward God and His plan for you.

This is the second requirement for true prayer - to recognize your need for God.

4. Matt. 6:7-15

We can do a whole lesson on the Lord's Prayer, but for now we want to talk about the third requirement for prayer, which is forgiveness.

We can't get very near to God without working on forgiving the people in our lives who have wounded us. And this is not a one-time event, like waking up one day and saying I'm forgiving this person for their meanness toward me. And some of you, I'm sure, have a lot to forgive. It's a process, like peeling an onion; layer after layer has to come off day by day. Or like dressing a wound which needs daily attention. When you can look back on the event and not feel the emotional pain, then you are making progress.

We are not expected to be able to forget. The Bible doesn't tell us to do that, but we do have to be in a forgiveness mode if God is going to hear our prayer and forgive us as He promises in the Lord's prayer.

A lack of forgiveness is the single greatest block to spiritual growth and can even cause physical sickness if one holds bitterness toward others in their heart (and body) and refuses to let go.

*****

After looking at three requirements for prayer, let's look at some of the ways we pray. We could say, "pray any way you can," but the Scriptures tell us about some specific ways of praying.

Here are Scriptures which refer to several:

5. Matt. 6:5-6

Entering into our "prayer closet" is the time when we can be most open and honest with God. The privacy of this time of prayer allows us to fully open our hearts to God with intercessory prayer, to tell Him all of our needs, to complain, whine and weep. This is the real you before the "real God" who wants you to be fully open with Him. God wants you to "cast all your cares upon Him for He care for you" as the Psalmist says. This is the time to talk to God and share every aspect of your life.

6. I Thess. 5:16-21

Pray without ceasing. Does this mean saying the Lord's prayer or any other prayer over and over again, or even just talking to God constantly?

Well, it could, but more likely the meaning is to keep the Lord's name and presence ever before you. "Practicing the presence of God" is the way the monks describe it. Just be aware of God in everything you do.

You have to make a real effort to practice this, as there are so many diversions today in our culture. Someone said that if the Devil doesn't get you by destruction, he will get you by distraction with the various media out there—the web, TV, Twitter, Facebook, etc. People are living their entire lives in a state of distraction and so utterly lost to themselves that they are at a loss as to what to do when alone without some sort of "noise" in the background. Stripping away the background noise of this civilization is essential to realizing you are never away from the presence of God; you're simply distracted from being aware of His presence.

7. I Kings 19:9-12

Did God come to Elijah in the storm, fire, or wind? No. He came to Him in a still small voice. This is instructive for another way to pray that enables us to listen to God. Christians have been doing this for centuries. Fr. Thomas Keating, in the many books he has written, has provided instruction in this way of listening to God, and I want to go over it with you. (See Appendix for the Centering Prayer handout.)

Read: Other Voices

Dear God, Help Me to Persevere in Prayer

Heavenly Father, I know I give up too soon by not trusting in Your steadfast love and Your wisdom for my life. I am certain at times that I have it all figured out and just need You to rubber stamp my own agenda. I am too impatient to wait for the unfolding of Your plans for me. I know You are longing for me to grow like You, and that means perseverance when I pray by waiting in stillness and faith to be conformed to Your Image. In the name of the Father, the Son and the Holy Spirit, I pray. Amen.

VOICES FROM THE BIBLE

Read Psalm 40:1-3. The Lord hears our prayers.
I waited patiently for the Lord...

1) Matt. 17:14-20   *The requirement for answers to prayer*
2) Mark 10:46-52   *Blind Bartimaeus does not give up*
3) Luke 11:5-13   *A persistent friend*
4) Luke 18:1-5   *A persistent widow*
5) 1 Thess. 5:16-22   *Pray without ceasing*
6) Eph. 6:18-20   *Supplications for others*

OTHER VOICES

The Spirit teaches me to yield my will entirely to the will of the Father. He opens my ear to wait in great gentleness and teachableness of soul for what the Father has day by day to speak and to teach. He reveals to me how union with God's will is union with God Himself; how entire surrender to God's will is the Father's claim, the Son's example, and the true blessedness of the soul.
-Andrew Murray

The truth of the matter is, we all come to prayer with a tangled mass of motives—altruistic and selfish, merciful and hateful, loving and bitter. Frankly, this side of eternity we will never unravel the good from the bad, the pure from the impure. But what I have come to see is that God is big enough to receive us with all our mixture. We do not have to be bright, or pure, or filled with faith, or anything. That is what grace means, and not only are we saved by grace, we live by it as well. And we pray by it.
-Richard Foster

God is interested in your prayers because He is interested in you. Whatever matters to you is a priority for His attention. Nothing in the universe matters as much to Him as what is going on in your life this day. You don't have to pester Him to get His attention. You don't have to spend hours on your knees or flail yourself or go without food to show Him you really mean business. He's your Father; He wants to hear what you have to say. In fact, He's waiting for you to call. –Bill Hybels

When we have opened ourselves in depth to God's compassionate but also radical transformation of our lives, something always happens within us. There is always some change on some level: a change in the understanding of the self, a change in health, a change in relationships, a change in habits, a change in compassionate and moral awareness.
-Flora Slossom Wuellner

YOUR VOICE

1) *Share an occasion when you were persistent in prayer.*
2) *What does "pray without ceasing" mean to you in your prayer life?*
3) *When you pray over and over without relenting, do you change God's mind, or do you yourself change?*
4) *What is the appropriate way to pray for others? Do you know what is best for them? How easy is it for you to totally surrender them to God?*
5) *What is the problem with the "Name it, claim it" school?*

COMMENTARY & DISCUSSION

Dear God, Help Me to Persevere in Prayer

Read Psalm 40:1

The Psalmist perseveres in patience. He believes the Lord has heard him as He draws him up out of the miry pit. Patience and perseverance must be an essential part of our prayer life. God is on a different time frame from us. He sees everything at once and not on a continuum. His time is not our time. This is why patience and perseverance are essential on our part and in this waiting, we have the opportunity to grow and open ourselves up to His will.

The final result of this process is that God has set the Psalmist's feet on a rock and given him a new song, perhaps not the old words of despair and defeat but a new one of joy, freedom and love.

What is the "rock" referred to by the Psalmist?

1. Matt. 17:14-20

The point of this passage is to have complete faith in God, not to move mountains. Jesus is reprimanding His disciples for their lack of faith.

We can pray until we are blue in the face, say every prayer we know, including the Lord's Prayer, but if we don't have faith that God hears our prayers and will answer them according to His will, in His time, and when we are ready, we are wasting our time.

A test of whether we truly have this faith is to check your attitude after you have prayed. Are you still worrying about the request you have made of God? Then you haven't really prayed. Are you at peace, surrendered, floating in the love of God? Then you have prayed. In short, if you are going to continue to worry, then don't bother to pray; if after you pray, you are at peace, then your prayers will bear fruit.

2. Mark 10:46-52

This is not strictly a passage about prayer, but in a way, it is, as Bartimaeus was calling on the Lord to be healed. The point is that he persisted, even when others rebuked him. The words he uses, "Jesus, Son of David, have mercy on me!" are a slight variation of the traditional prayer, "Lord Jesus Christ, have mercy on me," which Christians have prayed since Pentecost. And even though others tried to silence him, he did not give up. The result was that Jesus heard him and told the crowd to call him. Bartimaeus, in hastening to the Lord, left his mantle behind. Why? Perhaps because he had such faith that he would be healed that he knew he could return with his eyesight restored and pick it up.

How does this apply to our lives?

First, keep calling on God and keep praying for something you truly believe God wants: your healing, your salvation, the salvation of loved ones, and such desirable ends as these. Second, even though others may not support you in your requests, doubting they will be answered and telling you you're wasting your time, do not give up. Persevere as Bartimaeus did.

The reason we know the name of this blind man is that he was converted to the Lord and became a leader in the early church.

3. Luke 11:5-13

The Lord asks which of you would go to a friend in the middle of the night and bang on the door and ask for food for your visitor. In those times, the demand was even more inconvenient because people in those days slept in houses with a large wooden door with iron bars to keep out robbers and unwanted visitors. Everyone slept on a mat in a single room in the house. To get up and open the door would be to disturb and wake the whole family. Yet the Lord says that in spite of the inconvenience, the door would be opened if the insistence is strong enough. The word "importunity," which means "shameless insistence," is used in some translations. In other words, we are to go boldly to God in our prayers, demanding answers to them.

He goes on to elaborate and assures His listeners that if they ask, it will be given to them; if they seek, they will find; if they knock, the door will open.

To ask means you may not receive what you want, but it will be what God wants for you. What is your experience in this?

To seek may mean that you may not find your answer, but you will more likely find God. Whatever you truly seek, you will find. What you truly desire will come to you. What is your experience with regard to seeking? What do you truly desire?

To knock, again, implies persistence. The door may slowly open, and it may take years for that to happen. To pray for wounded family members who need to change as well as for our own spiritual maturity may take decades before we see results, but we do not stop knocking at that door.

Your experience?

4. Luke 18:1-5

This is another parable on persistence and not giving up. Why did Jesus put several parables with the same message before His followers? Because persistence is so important and so necessary a part of our prayer life. This old widow was not intimidated by the judge, and she did not relent. And she finally wore him out. We're not saying we can wear God out. This is not the point of the parable. The point is not to stop praying, regardless of lack of an answer, because if the parable is true, God will eventually hear and respond. He will restore the "righteousness" that may have been taken away from us.

However, to persevere in prayer may mean to accept the fact that we may not be ready to receive what we are praying for. Total surrender to God's will is the other side of the coin of perseverance m prayer.

5. I Thess. 5:16-22

Some translations read "without ceasing" and some read "constantly", but the point is never to stop praying. Does that mean we walk around saying the Lord's Prayer all day? No. Rather, it means to keep the awareness of the Lord always before us, whatever we are doing. This is not easy in a culture which is constantly trying to sell us something or distract us with cell phones, social media, etc. It takes a lot of discipline and love of God to truly focus on Him at all times.

To pray without ceasing, or try to constantly keep the Lord in your thoughts, will change you. As you draw closer to God, you will realize that He is already close to you. You will find yourself guided by Him in everything you do. The result will be the joy that Paul talks about. Unceasing prayer and constant joy go hand in hand. Further, gratitude will become part of your life. That's why Paul puts these three together. Prayer, joy and gratitude have always characterized the focused and devout Christian.

How hard is it for you to do this? What tools are provided for us to pray without ceasing?

6. Ephesians 6:18-20

Another reminder to pray constantly. Paul was a prayer warrior, and he wanted all of his followers to do the same because that is the path to transformation. He further admonishes us to pray for each other (the saints, in his view, referred to all followers of Christ). Again, perseverance is part of prayer. We do not give up praying for ourselves and for others, and not just for friends and neighbors but also for our enemies. This is the mark of the true Christian.

He refers to himself as an "ambassador in chains," referring to the fact that he is in prison. And yet some of his more profound writings come from his time in prison.

Do you feel that you have a special opportunity for spiritual growth while here in jail? Are there are some special tasks you can accomplish while here? Maybe keeping a journal while in prison to write down your daily thoughts and prayers? Resolutions for leading a different life when you leave?

Read: Other Voices

Dear God, Help Me to Pray the Psalms

Dear God, I know the Psalms are the prayers of the Church, and they can provide me with the words I need when I praise You, draw near to You, grieve, lose hope, and receive Your guidance. Help me to turn to the Psalms more and more as I seek comfort, guidance, hope, love and nearness to You. In the name of the Father, the Son and the Holy Spirit. Amen.

VOICES FROM THE BIBLE

Read Psalm 150. Praise the Lord!
Let everything that has breath Praise the Lord!

1)	Psalm 136 - Praise	*For His steadfast love endures forever!*
2)	Psalm 63 - Food	*My soul is feasted with marrow and fat*
3)	Psalm 42 - Longing	*As the hart longs for flowing stream.*
4)	Psalm 139 - Guidance	*And lead me in the way everlasting*
5)	Psalms 91 - Care	*He will cover you with his feathers*

OTHER VOICES

In many ways, the Psalms are at the heart of the Bible, or at least at the start of important places in the Bible. Not surprisingly, then, one finds the Gospels portraying Jesus frequently turning to the Psalms to experience peace in the desperate moment of dying (Luke 23:46; 31:3), as earlier in difficult times of controversy (Matt. 22:42-44; Ps. 110:1) or temptation (Matt 4:3-11; Ps. 44:23); or for inculcating trust in God's loving care (Luke 12:22; Ps. 55:23).
-Carroll Stuhlmueller

The book of Psalms provides the most reliable theological, pastoral and liturgical resource given us in the biblical tradition. In season and out of season, generation after generation, faithful women and men turn to the Psalms as a most helpful resource for conversation with God about things that matter most.
-Walter Brueggeman

The Psalms are a vast temple in which God is worshipped. Each individual Psalm is like a room in the temple, full of God's presence but not exhausting it. Praising God in one Psalm, we hear echoes of songs from other rooms. The Psalms in their totality are the "script" for the people of God, themselves a temple wherein God is worshipped, so that in the singing of the Psalms the two temples come together.
-Laurence Kriegshauser

The Psalter is one of the most important books for all Christians and why each of them, whatever his circumstances may be, finds in it Psalms and words which are appropriate to the circumstances in which he finds himself and meets his needs as adequately as if they were composed exclusively for his sake, and in such a way that he himself could not improve on them nor could find or desire any better Psalms or words.
-German Psalter (1528)

YOUR VOICE

1) *Do the Psalms lead you to God?*
2) *How is God portrayed in the Psalms?*
3) *In what ways do the Psalms connect with your life experiences?*
4) *How are our life experiences and those of the Psalmist different?*
5) *Where have you heard God's voice in the Psalms that apply to today?*
6) *When do you experience God in such a way that you want to shout out words of praise or give expression to wonder?*

COMMENTARY & DISCUSSION

Dear God, Help me to Pray the Psalms

Introduction

The primary theme in all of the Psalms is the relationship of the Psalmist to God and the devout love which flows between them. This takes many forms: longing for God, need for guidance, comfort, and expression of hate against God's enemies. But the focus is always on God, His intimate involvement in our lives, and our struggle to be faithful to Him.

Isn't this what we all want to spend our time doing? Struggling to be faithful and loving to the One who first loved us? A faithful and regular reading of the Psalms can help us to do this. You may want to memorize sections of some Psalms to guide, comfort and keep God close to you.

Read Psalm 150

This Psalm is the great Hallelujah, the final one of three Psalms of praises which end the book of Psalms. It is a call to all the voices in heaven and on earth as well as the musical instruments used in the temple to praise God because in praising God, the meaning of the world is fulfilled. This is our first responsibility to God, first in our prayer, first in our thoughts and first in our lives if we are to live close to Him and affirm Him as our Lord and Master. His praise should always be on our lips.

How is this working in your life?

1. Psalm 136

This beautiful Psalm begins with celebrating the wondrous works God has done in Creation to the deliverance of the Israelites from Egypt, to remembrance of us in our misery, to giving food to all flesh. It expresses the entire range of God's goodness and mercy. It was sung by the Israelites at the harvest feast, which celebrated the blessing of the bounty of food given by God each year. Interspersed between each of these hymns which were probably sung by the priest is the response, "and His steadfast love endures forever."

The alternative singing between the priest and the choir is practiced in some churches today when the priest offers a prayer and the people/choir respond by singing, "Lord have mercy."

Do you celebrate/praise Him for His steadfast love at every blessing that comes your way? Should we praise Him only for His blessings?

2. Psalm 63

In this Psalm, the poet sees God as his food. That has come down to the Church today when we see the Eucharist as in some mysterious way being the Body and Blood of Christ. The writer's soul thirsts for God. He feasts on God's presence as on marrow and fat—the most sustaining part of meat.

He also meditates on God in his bed at night. Because God is his helper, he sings for joy in the shadow of His wings. Could this be the Psalmist's time of prayer? His soul clings to God; God upholds him.

This is the voice of one who has a very intimate and devout relationship to God.

How do we achieve such intimacy? Could that develop with just occasional prayer or attending Church only on Sunday? Probably not. This requires great devotion to God, daily prayer and focusing our mind on God through the day. Unceasing prayer is what Paul recommends for staying close to God.

3. Psalm 42

In contrast to Psalm 63, Psalm 42 reflects someone who feels very distant from God and is longing to be near Him. As a deer pants for water, so he pants for God.

How does it feel to be really thirsty? You'll do anything to quench it. That's how this Psalmist felt about God. His great need for God causes him to weep to calm himself. Further, he recalls memories of being in the temple with the festal celebration. His soul is cast down. Finally, the only solution is to wait for God. His strong faith will sustain him until he renews his relationship with God. The psalmist saw this relationship with God as the most important aspect of his life. His God is the living God, and the Psalmist lives to come into communion with Him.

Have you ever felt this way? That God was very far from you and that you hungered and thirsted to be closer to Him? Do you have the faith to believe that He will make Himself known to you if you wait patiently in trust and love?

4. Psalm 139

This overwhelmingly beautiful Psalm sees God as all present, all knowing, and all creating. The Psalmist is in awe and wonder at the incomprehensible greatness of God. There's no way he can flee from His presence, no way he can comprehend His greatness, and no way can he understand His knowledge of the most intimate aspects of his being. "Thou didst knit me together in my mother's womb."

He moves from wonder at his conception to the awareness that God knows the number of his days—how long he will live.

He then affirms his hatred for those who hate God. God's enemies are his enemies. It is for the sake of God that he rejects those who shamefully abuse God's holy name.

Then finally, since God is the Creator of all, who alone can lead one to the truth, he asks God to search him, know his thoughts, test him as to whether he walks in evil ways, "and lead me in the way everlasting."

What an awesome Psalm! How can we not trust the One who knows us so well, who created us in our mother's womb, who knows how long we will live?

How can we open our hearts and souls so that He can lead us in the "way everlasting"?

5. Psalm 91

In this Psalm, the writer expresses total trust of God's care in every danger or evil that can come his way. He need not fear the terrors of the night, flying arrows, pestilence and enemies of all types. Because of his trust, angels will guard him, wild animals will not touch him. Because of his love for God, he will be delivered, God will respond when he calls and will give him long life and salvation.

The true aim of this Psalm is to show that the living relationship with God by someone who trusts in Him will result in God's protection of him in all the affliction and perils of his life.

The requirement is to dwell in the shadow of the Almighty and to cleave to Him in love. This trust in God leaves behind every earthly fear, every human doubt, and lifts us up above the depressing realities of life to the certainty of a faith which enables one to endure life and master it.

However, as Christians, are we always protected in every situation? Do we not experience some of the evils the Psalmist describes?

Yes, and this is where surrender and submission to God's will comes in. The point of the Psalm is to have total trust and faith in God in all circumstances, and when the bad things happen, to know and have faith that He is with you and will see you through whatever comes.

Do the bad things that happen to you destroy your faith in God? How do you maintain a strong faith, when your world is crumbling about you?

Read: Other Voices

Resource for commentary is drawn from *The Psalms*, Artur Weiser, Westminster Press, Philadelphia, 1962.

Prayer: Doorway to God

O Heavenly King, the Comforter, the Spirit of Truth, who art everywhere and fillest all things, treasury of blessings and giver of life. Come and abide in us, cleanse us from every impurity and save our souls O Good One.

VOICES FROM THE BIBLE

Read Psalm 55. A Song of Anguish
Give ear to my prayer, O God, and hide not thyself from my supplication.

1) Isaiah 40:28-31 — *Those who wait upon the Lord*
2) Heb. 10:19-24 — *Let us bravely come before God*
3) Matt. 6:5-13 — *The model for all prayer*
4) Phil. 4:6-9 — *No requests off limits*
5) Matt. 18:19-20 — *United in prayer*
6) Eph 3:14-19 — *Our prayer for each other*
7) II Cor. 3:12-18 — *The fruit of prayer*

OTHER VOICES

"Prayer changes things," people say. It also changes us. The latter goal is the more imperative. The primary purpose of prayer is to bring us into such a life of communion with the Father that, by the power of the Spirit, we are increasingly conformed to the image of the Son.
-Richard Foster

…silence is not the mere absence of speech. It is listening to God, receiving the word He communicates to us in His creation and in the history of salvation. It is entering into communion with His superabundant life, a life of mutual knowledge and love. It is speaking with God as one would speak with a friend with words and without words at that point where all the partial words come together in the reality of pure communion.
-Thomas Keating

Prayer is the laying aside of thoughts.
-Evagrius

O gracious and holy Father, give us wisdom to perceive Thee, intelligence to understand Thee, diligence to seek Thee, eyes to behold Thee, a heart to meditate upon Thee, and a life to proclaim Thee, through the power of the Spirit of Jesus Christ our Lord..
-Benedict of Nursia

"Not my preacher, not my teacher, but it's me, O Lord, standin' in the need of prayer."
-Gospel song

YOUR VOICE

1. *Do you find it difficult to pray? Why?*
2. *Do you use some prayers written by others? If so, are they helpful?*
3. *Why is silence essential as part of your prayer time?*
4. *Someone said that prayer should consist of asking, thanksgiving, and praise. Do you agree? What else might one include in prayer?*
5. *Do you feel changed after you pray?*

COMMENTARY & DISCUSSION

Prayer: Doorway to God

Read Psalm 55

1. Isaiah 40:28-31

This passage describes God giving power to the faint and increasing strength to those who have none. The condition for this is that we WAIT on the Lord. What happens in this passage for those who wait for the Lord? They gain their strength, they mount up with wings as eagles, they run and are not weary, they walk and do not faint.

If we view this in spiritual terms, we can see prayer, especially silent prayer, as a form of waiting on the Lord. We can then have the confidence that He will strengthen us, enable us to mount up with wings of joy, to do His bidding and walk in His way.

What are some other results of "waiting" on the Lord? How difficult is it to sit and wait when this involves total surrender and laying aside our own agenda?

2. Heb. 10:19-24

What does this passage mean when the author says that Christ opened the curtain with His flesh? It refers to Christ's Crucifixion and Resurrection, which tore down the curtain in the Temple that separated the people from the priest. This is because Christ becomes the great High Priest, and the Jewish priest no longer has to go behind the curtain once a year to offer a sacrifice for the sins of the people. We who have been baptized can individually go to Christ and confess our sins and be forgiven. Then we will be able to love each other and do the good works we are called to do. The "Day" referred to is the Second Coming, which the early church members assumed would be in their lifetimes.

One aspect of our prayer, then, should be confession and seeking forgiveness. In some churches, the priest stands in the place of the congregation and listens to your confession, since, originally, early Christians confessed to the whole church. Today, in other churches, persons can seek counsel for confession, or confess their sins one to another. Support groups such as AA, NA and other groups can provide an opportunity to share your guilt and remorse.

How difficult is it for you to confess your sins? Do you think it is necessary? Why or why not?

3. Matt. 6:5-13

The disciples were trained in Jewish prayer and were eager to learn more from their new Master as to how He would have them pray; thus, He taught them the "Lord's Prayer." He used the term Abba—a familiar term for God (similar to our use of "Daddy") not used before. It reflects an intimacy with

God that Jesus modeled and instituted. At the same time, He affirmed the holiness (hallowed) of His name. He prayed that His kingdom would come, that the very life of God the Father would be manifested over all the earth and, further, that His will would be done not only on earth but also over the entire cosmos. He then instructed His listeners to ask for nourishment on a daily basis. This could mean both spiritual and physical bread—both essential to our lives. God knows that we need both.

We should ask forgiveness and expect it only if we are in the process of forgiving others. We are blocked in receiving God's forgiveness if we are not forgiving toward others. Lack of forgiveness is a major block to spiritual growth, and that is why our Lord put it at the heart of the Lord's Prayer.

He also instructs us to ask the Father not to put temptation in our way, not to put us in situations we cannot handle, where the evil one rules, and to keep us from the one who would keep us from God.

The power of this prayer is not in the specific words. The power is in the One to whom we pray. We can make the same petitions using other words. They should include glorifying God, doing His will, asking for daily needs, forgiveness, and supplication to protect us from the evil one.

When we pray this prayer which is so familiar, we sometimes forget the meaning, so occasionally try using other words to prompt you to really think of what you are asking.

(Bring other translations of the Lord's prayer and hand them out.) How would you put the Lord's Prayer into your own words?

4. Phil. 4:6-9

The Apostle Paul says, "Always rejoice." This should constantly be a part of our prayer.

Why? Because of what Christ has done for us.

Do not be anxious. Someone said, "Suffering is inevitable; anxiety is optional."

Make your requests known to God through prayer and supplication, and if you do this, He may not give you exactly what you ask for, when you ask for it, but He will give you a peace that is beyond imagining. It's as though God is saying, "you tell me everything on your heart and in your mind that you need or are concerned about, and while I'm working on it, I will give you a peace beyond all you expected." Of course, this involves complete surrender and trust that God is looking after everything.

How difficult is this? What are "helps" to do this?

Paul goes on to urge us to keep our minds on what is true, honorable, pure, lovely, gracious, excellent and worthy of praise. Keep your mind filled with such thoughts. How difficult is this to do today when we are bombarded with the images and words of TV, social media, twitter, and daily news?

This is a major task in today's culture. It takes worship, prayer, Bible reading and quiet time, yet this is the narrow road that our Lord reminds us is the way to the Kingdom.

What are other lifestyle habits you can develop to keep your mind focused on good thoughts?

5. Matt. 18:19-20

If any two people agree on earth about anything they ask, it will be done for them by the Father in heaven, and when two or three gather in His name, He is there with them.

Of course, the request must be harmonious with His will. Asking for material wants (not needs) is an insult to God. We must be discerning in what is good for our souls and those of our loved ones and pray accordingly.

A group of men at Folsom Prison got together and prayed silently for a year, and certainly they were united in their desire to be released and not return. When they were released after a year, not one returned, and the recidivism rate at Folsom is 80%.

What is your experience in praying with others? Do you find it helpful?

6. Eph. 3:14-19

This is one of the most beautiful prayers for the faithful in the Apostle Paul's writings. Bending of the knee was not normally done unless one was especially concerned for those for whom one was praying.

He asks that they may be:

- Strengthened with might through the Spirit in the inner man.

- Rooted and grounded in love and have the power to know the love of Christ (this is power of the heart beyond head knowledge).

- Filled with all the fullness of God.

What a powerful prayer, one we should pray for all those people in our lives—family, friends and enemies.

How difficult is this, especially prayer for the enemy?

7. II Cor. 3:12-18

Paul is speaking of the Old Covenant and refers to the occasion when Moses had to put a veil over his face after he came down the mountain after receiving the Ten Commandments because the Israelites could not view the fading splendor.

But the New Covenant in Christ takes away the veil. By gazing at Christ with our spiritual eyes, beholding His glory, we are all being changed into His likeness from one degree of glory to another.

This is the whole purpose of Christ's coming: to transform us into His likeness. This is why His Church exists, why we have Scriptures and are told to pray. As we are transformed, then we are able to love our brothers, sisters, and even our enemies. We can then begin to love with the love with which we have been loved.

One of the early saints said, "God became man that man might become like God." This is the Christian faith and the means of our salvation.

Read: Other Voices

Warfare in Prayer: Winning Battles God's Way

Lord, we know that just as you struggled in prayer in the Garden, we also struggle not only in prayer, but in setting aside time for prayer. And when the Big Three—world, flesh, devil—stand to oppose us, help us to be strong in the Lord and in the strength of His might. When we stand to pray, let us be confident that You are standing with us to help us conquer those forces that would keep us from You. In the name of the Father, the Son and the Holy Spirit. Amen

VOICES FROM THE BIBLE

Read Psalm 142. I cry to the Lord!
Bring me out of prison that I may give thanks to thy name!

1) Exodus 14:5-18 — *The Lord is a warrior winning battles*
2) Luke 22:31-34; 54-62 — *The Lord encourages us in prayer*
3) Ephesians 6:10-20 — *God provides armor for the battle*
4) Luke 18:3-5 — *We are urged to persevere*
5) II Cor. 12:1-10 — *Paul was persistent in prayer*
6) Heb. 4:14-16 — *Jesus was tempted as we are*
7) James 4:1-10 — *God sets conditions for answering our prayer*

OTHER VOICES

Remember four elements in making a request to God: Relate to God first. Know who God is and know that your relationship with Him is the basis for your request. Request from God. Recognize that He is the one who can meet this request. Reason with God. Talk to Him about the request, what it means to Him and to you. Rejoice before God. Celebrate His promises and answers.

In winning battles God's way, we start with the fact that God is God—Jesus is Lord. Jesus is the victor who conquered all on the Cross. We agree with those truths by humbling ourselves under His mighty hand (I Peter 5:6), receiving and putting on His armor. He pours out grace on the humble heart and enables us to stand strong in Him, in His armor. This means receiving his Word and walking in His Spirit day by day, listening carefully, following closely and resisting firmly. God's Word fortifies faith and enables us to quench fiery darts so they do not penetrate our thinking or affect our walking. The Word of God thus equips us with a firm faith. We stand with firm footing and can thereby wield the sword of the Spirit in prayer—always praying in the Spirit, depending on Him to guide us and continually strengthen and establish us (I Peter 5:6- 11).

Merimnaó is translated "to be anxious." The word is actually a combination of two Greek words: *merizo*, which means to divide or distribute (as Jesus divided the loaves and fish—Mark 6:41) and *nous*, referring to the thoughts. *Merimnaó* pictures a mind divided, thoughts distracted and going in many directions rather than focused and fixed on what God wants in thought and action. Jesus often spoke of not being anxious. In Matthew 6:25-31, He warned about worrying over food and clothing.

Jesus rebuked Martha over being "worried and bothered about so many things" (Luke 10:41). As Philippians 4:6-7 reveals, instead of worrying, He wants us praying, looking to Him to meet the need or give needed direction.

YOUR VOICE

1) *What battles do you face in prayer? Is it hard to begin? Difficult to stay focused? On the basis on this lesson, what can you do about it?*
2) *How can you use the armor of God described in Ephesians 6 to help you to pray?*
3) *In what ways does praying help you to develop a relationship with God?*
4) *Do you feel at times that you are fighting God instead of the devil in prayer?*
5) *When praying about a particular concern, is it more important to focus on the problem or on the solution?*

This lesson title and Other Voices were drawn from pp.149-167 in *Praying God's Way*, Rich Shepherd, AMG Publishers, Chattanooga, TN, 2005.

COMMENTARY & DISCUSSION

Warfare in Prayer: Winning Battles God's way

Introduction

The first thing we have to say about prayer is that prayer is the process of developing a relationship with God. Anything that draws us to prayer—praise, intercession, release of pain, and suffering of any other kind—helps us to develop that relationship.

However, the Devil wants us to avoid prayer because he knows it will bring us into deeper communion with God. So one way of looking at prayer is as warfare. Someone once pointed out that when you begin to pray, all the demons line up on one side and all the angels on the other. That's why prayer can sometimes be a real struggle and why we often put off praying. But this lesson points us to the reality that God is directing this battle, and we can win it by trusting that He is on our side in this spiritual warfare.

Read Psalm 142

When we are really serious about prayer, we cry out to the Lord. We don't just mumble some words. We complain to Him, tell Him our troubles. We feel at times there is no escape, no one cares for us, there is no refuge. Do you sometimes experience this?

But as the Psalmist says, the Lord is your refuge and will deliver you. He will bring you out of the prison you are in both in spirit and in body. The support you have from others will surround you, and God will deal bountifully with you. This is the promise of the One fighting your battles with you.

1. Ex. 14:5-18

You know this story. The Lord fought for the Israelites. The Lord will fight for you and sometimes you just have to wait, trust and be still. Sometimes when the battle overwhelms us, as did the threat to the Israelites from the Egyptian army, we have to leave it all to God.

What are some ways you can practice stillness, waiting, and surrendering to God? What tools does God give us to enable us to do this?

2. Luke 22:31-34, 54-62

The Lord warns Peter that Satan will be after him. Why? Peter (from *petra*, which means "rock") was potentially a strong disciple, which is why Jesus called him a "rock." Satan especially wants to bring him down.

The more spiritually sensitive you are, the greater your potential for growth in God, and the more the Devil will pursue you. That may be the reason some of you are here. God may want you for a special task, and the Devil knows it, so he will do battle against you. However, as with Peter, Jesus is praying for you. He prayed that Peter's faith would not fail, and the Lord assured him that when he had conquered the Devil, he then would be able to strengthen his brothers.

When you have been through this trial by fire and your strength is greater, you, too, can help others. You will be tested by temptation, and even if you fail, God can raise you up to be a stronger, more serviceable follower of Him.

Peter denied his Lord three times and yet became the greatest of the apostles and the leader of the other apostles.

How do you deal with temptation?

3. Ephesians 6:10-20

We put on armor to prepare for battle. And the "battle" for our salvation is the most significant one of our life. And God provides all that we need for this. Putting on armor for the Christian is putting on Christ. He is our shield and defender. Putting on Christ enables us to withstand all the schemes of the Devil, his deceptions and lies, darts of discouragement and doubt, arrows of depression. This is not a physical battle which draws blood. It is a spiritual battle in which your soul is at stake.

How do we put on Christ? Ask the Holy Spirit.

What are some other types of "armor" you can put on?

4. Luke 18:3-5

Giving up on prayer or just mumbling words to get through is a real temptation. We get weary and want to abandon the effort. This parable is on not giving up. The reason is that our persistent prayer does not change God. He always wants the best for us. Our persistent prayer changes us. It changes us because the more often we come to God, the more we become like Him and see our own lives the way He sees them. We enter into harmony with God's will for us. Further, persistent prayer increases our love for God and, as a result, we become more loving to others.

To be persistent and steady, you need a prayer rule (rule means regular). Part of a rule means to pray on a regular basis at a certain time of day, preferably in the morning before breakfast on an empty stomach. Your mind will be more focused at that time.

Your prayer should include adoration: loving, praising and thanking God; confession of what you have done wrong and determination to improve; asking for your personal needs, strength, insight, guidance, help with problems, ways to grow in Christ, and intercession for others; and finally, a time of stillness when you can just be quiet and listen to God. (Hand out Prayer Rule. See Appendix)

How do you pray?

5. II Cor. 12:1-10

Paul persevered in prayer. He was so close to Christ and prayed so devoutly that he experienced a vision. So he would not be too elated by this vision, the Lord sent him a "thorn in the flesh," which He refused to remove in spite of Paul's asking three times for release. Instead, Christ led him to the realization that His power was perfected in weakness. Paul accepted this and acknowledged that "when I am weak (in my own power) I am strong (in God's power)."

What does this mean and what does this tell us about unanswered prayer?

Perhaps it means that when some problem is not solved by the Lord after prayer, we lean on Him more, rely on His strength, accept what we cannot change, and look to Him to give us the strength to continue. (See the Serenity Prayer in the Appendix.)

Response?

6. Heb. 4:14-16

Hebrews 4:14 speaks of Jesus as our "great high priest who has passed through the heavens" and points to His powerful victory over sin, death and the Devil. Further, He is a high priest marked not only by power, but also by compassion. He can "sympathize with our weaknesses, since He was tempted in all things as we are." He understands the heat of the battles we face. Today He sits on a throne of grace to which we can come and receive His mercy "to help in time of need"—exactly the grace we need at the time we need it.

With such a powerful Intercessor, should we not be confident that our spiritual battles can be won?

7. James 4:1-10

James warns us that if we pray just for materials goods over and above what we need, or for status or power, God is not going to honor these prayers. Prayer is establishing a relationship with the One who is most concerned for our soul. The prayers He hears and honors are the ones having to do with our salvation or with the salvation of others. Or out of love, if we pray for physical healing for others or for ourselves so that we can be better servants, He will hear and honor these prayers. You may be praying to be released from prison so you can return to the work you are to do in this world and enter back into relationship with spouse, children, family. God honors such prayers and will answer them in His time and according to His will.

Friendship with the world is enmity with God. What does that mean? To preoccupy ourselves with the things our culture offers—material wealth, sexual indulgence, violence, drugs—will alienate us from God. James says, "He yearns jealously over the Spirit which he has made to dwell within us." He wants that Spirit directed to Him.

Humility is essential. Humble yourself before God, and he will exalt you. Humility means to realize how needy you are. Bring those needs to God. He will hear you and elevate your spirit by confirming His love for you

Surrender to God is the foundation of every prayer and the key invocation in the Lord's Prayer: "Thy will be done." What could be better than His perfect will in our lives?

This should be our constant and unceasing prayer as we walk our Christian journey.

Read: Other Voices

SUFFERING

How God uses Our Sufferings

"Suffering is inevitable; anxiety is optional."

God, we know that everything that comes our way, whether good or bad, can be used by You to draw us closer to You. We ask that You would help us see Your hand in all things, allowing for us those things that would turn us away from the world and toward Your Face. And regardless of what happens to us, let us continue to trust that we are being carried in the everlasting arms of Your love. In the name of the one who suffered and died for us, Your Son, Jesus Christ. Amen

VOICES FROM THE BIBLE

Read Psalm 6. Supplication in a time of trial
O, Lord, heal me for my bones are troubled. My soul also is greatly troubled.

1. Mark 15:16-39, Luke 23:39-43 — *Jesus is crucified*
2. Job 42: 1-6 — *Job comes into communion with God*
3. John 9:1-7 — *That the work of God might be revealed*
4. II Cor. 1:3-7 — *God comforts us in our sufferings*
5. James 1:2-4; 12-14 — *Be joyful in trials*
6. I Peter 5:6-19 — *After you have suffered a while*
7. Hebrews 12:1-13 — *Steady your weary hands and trembling knees*

OTHER VOICES

In summary, Jesus did three things to solve the problem of suffering. First, He came. He suffered with us. He wept. Second, in becoming man, He transformed the meaning of our suffering: it is now part of His work of redemption. Our birth pangs become birth pangs for heaven, not only for ourselves but also for those we love. Third, He died and rose. Dying, he destroyed the ultimate evil—death—and opened heaven to us. Rising, He transformed death from a hole into a door, from an end to a beginning.

We began with a mystery, not just of suffering but of suffering in a world supposedly created by a loving God. How to get God off the hook? (of allowing so much suffering, in spite of His love). The answer is Jesus. Jesus is not God off the hook but God on the hook. That's why the doctrine of the divinity of Christ is crucial. If that is not God there on the cross but only a good man, then God is not on the hook, on the cross, in our suffering. And if God is not on the hook, how could He sit there in heaven and ignore our tears? There is one good reason for not believing in God: evil. And God Himself has answered this objection, not by words but in deeds and in tears. Jesus is the tears of God. -Peter Kreeft

YOUR VOICE

1. *How can you not "waste your suffering"?*
2. *Can you use your experience in jail to help others? How?*
3. *What/Who do you need most when you are going through hard times?*
4. *When are you closest to God? In good times or in bad times? Why?*

Kreeft, Peter. *Making Sense Out of Suffering*, Servant Books, Ann Arbor, MI. 1986

COMMENTARY & DISCUSSION

How God Uses our Sufferings

Read Psalm 6

This is a man who is suffering and who turned to God for help. He complained of weakness as both his body and soul were sick. When the body is out of sorts, everything else looks bleak.

"Deliver me for the sake of your steadfast love." What role does love have in our healing?

There was a study done of low-income women in California who returned to a clinic again and again with one malady after the other. Someone decided to do research into their backgrounds and early childhood. They learned that these women, early in life, had been abused and rejected; they did not get enough love when growing up. When counseling and addressing these issues took place, they didn't get sick as often. Apparently, enough love can both heal you and prevent you from getting sick so often.

The Psalmist, in making his plea for help, warns God that, "if I die, how can I praise or serve you?" Finally, he declares that God has heard his supplication, so apparently healing has taken place. Thus, we can be assured that the Lord hears our weeping and will hopefully turn back our suffering and our sickness.

1. Mark 15:16-39; Luke 23:39-43

God suffered. No one has or ever will suffer like He suffered in the form of His son Jesus Christ. There are at least three ways in which this occurred:

1. Physical torment. Probably the most cruel way a person could die was on a cross. It is a long, terrible, excruciating death. The person finally dies because their lungs fill up with water; they literally drown in their own fluids.
2. Rejection by His own people. The religious leaders forced Rome to crucify him because they feared that He would bring about the end of their religion.
3. God forsook him. "My God, My God, why have you forsaken me?" God did forsake Him, because He literally went down into hell. He went to the place where Satan reigns.

God raised up Christ and by so doing overcame death. So we no longer fear death because Christ conquered death by death. Because he suffered so, our suffering can have meaning if we see it through His eyes.

Our Lord told us to "take up your cross and follow me." Our cross is our suffering, but unless we "follow" Him, i.e. worship, prayer, and Bible study, our cross will be so heavy that it will bury us. In following Him, our cross can become a means of growth. Jail can be a" womb of transformation," according to a former jail chaplain.

How can we allow God to bring good out of our own suffering?

2. Job 42:1-6

Satan suggested that if God caused great suffering to come upon His servant Job, that Job "would curse Him to His face." God allowed it, and Job was stripped of everything: family, lands, property and health. But he still would not deny God. He did argue with God, however, for 41 chapters about why he was suffering. In the Old Testament, if a person was good, they were made wealthy. So to have all his wealth taken away would indicate some evil in that person. It seemed to Job that God had found a flaw in him and was making him suffer, and since he felt he was not guilty, he wanted to know why God had taken everything away from him. God replied to him, essentially saying to him, "Will you condemn me that you may be justified?"

In the final chapter, 42, God enters into personal communion with Job and offers him His love. Job responds by saying, "I despise (root of the word may be related to a word meaning "to melt into nothing") myself." Job "melts" in the presence of God's love. His heart overrules his head and he has no more questions.

If we were to know why we suffer, what would that knowledge matter? But if we know the infinite, incredible, incomprehensible love of God for us, somehow the answer to the question is not important. We move from our head to our heart, from information to communion, as Job did.

Have you had an experience of this, moving from your head (need to know) to your heart (trusting in God to work it all out)?

3. John 9:1-7

The Jews believed at that time that all suffering was caused by sin. It wasn't that the parents or the man sinned but that the works of God were revealed through suffering. So Jesus moved the emphasis from looking for someone to blame (the Jewish position) to an opportunity for healing and transformation, which was why He came to earth.

We, too often, look for someone to blame for our sins, negative behavior, and/or suffering. That may be the case if you were sexually abused as a child or someone manipulated you into taking drugs. But even if that is the case, we shouldn't dwell on blame or even wallow around in remorse. We must look at the source of our transformation, which is Christ.

Can you look back and see how your suffering or sickness has revealed the work of the Lord to you, has shown you how God is working in your life? How did you deal with what you have been dealt?

4. II Cor. 1:3-7

Henri Nouwen, a Roman Catholic priest who worked at a center in Canada for people with developmental disabilities, wrote a book called *The Wounded Healer*. In it he discusses that, quite often, the people who have a suffered a lot, transcended it, and have grown as a result can be very helpful to others who are suffering. People who go to treatment centers for alcohol or drugs find that the leaders of AA or NA who have been down the same road and have recovered are the most effective leaders of such groups. Bill Wilson who wrote "The Big Book for Alcoholic Anonymous," which has helped millions to recover from addition, was himself a recovering addict. So in your jail experience and/or your recovery from addiction, you can be a special help to others.

Don't waste your sufferings. Go to the Lord with it, do everything you can to be healed, and you will become His minister, His word to others who are going through what you have been through.

Can you begin to see that your response to what you are going through can be useful to another person who may have experienced something similar?

5. James 1:2-4, 12-14

We are to be joyful when we meet trials, knowing this testing will produce perseverance. We are blessed when we endure trial, for if we stand the test, we will receive the crown of life.

God tempts no one. He does not send evil. Rather we get ourselves into our own messes. Sin has its own consequences. God didn't run Adam and Eve out of the Garden. He told them the rules and asked for obedience. They refused, so they suffered the consequences of their actions. If we acknowledge our sins and turn to God, He can work through our predicaments to bring about our salvation.

Sin gives birth to suffering, but if we can learn from our sufferings, it is that very experience which prompts us to change and move to a higher level of growth. For example, you get addicted to drugs, then you get caught for trying to keep up that habit through some criminal behavior and end up here. You are released and, if fortunate, you get into a rehab center. You will be far more wise and more valuable to other people due to this experience. Dorothy Sayers, a British writer who did a translation of a book called *The Divine Comedy*, says that Adam, fallen and redeemed, is far dearer to God than Adam before the fall. Why do you think that is the case?

Christ was crucified by sinful men for sinful reasons but by His unjust suffering, He condemns sin and opens for us the door to eternal life. God is at His most glorious on the Cross because it was through that—an act of love beyond all comprehension—that He opened for us the door to paradise.

6. I Peter 5:6-19

Surrender all to God, Give Him all your cares. The Devil is roaring around seeking to grab us at any minute. The closer you get to God, the more the Devil is going to attempt to make you slip up. But Peter assures us that "after you have suffered a little while the God of all grace will Himself restore, strengthen and establish you." In other words, don't give up or give into cynicism due to your suffering.

What can you do as you wait for God to "restore, strengthen and establish" you?

7. Hebrews 12:1-13

This letter was written at a time of great suffering and persecution for Christians, so the focus is on the fact that suffering can serve as a discipline, the experience of which can make us more devoted disciples. God does not bother with those who are not His true sons. He only disciplines—allows growth-producing suffering—for His true sons. He allows to happen to us what is necessary to benefit us the most spiritually. He doesn't send it but rather sometimes allows us to suffer for our sins to wake us up and help us grow. Do you see how your suffering is producing spiritual growth? Share.

Suffering without God can be hell. Suffering with God can be pure joy in the sense that God is closest to us at the point of our greatest suffering. Remember the thief on the cross who asked our Lord to "Remember me when you come into your kingdom"? He was immediately promised that he would be with Christ in paradise. His extreme suffering, in turning to God, brought him into paradise. And, incidentally, he was the first person to enter paradise.

Turn to God in the hard times, and it can be a time of deep inner peace, and you will gain a sense that you are in greater communion with Him. The more we suffer affliction, if we stay close to God, the more we become like Him who suffered beyond all imagining.

How then do we turn suffering from a burden into great spiritual growth?

1. Prayer: without ceasing morning, noon and night.
2. Patience: endure what comes, looking always to the Christ. Ask yourself: "What can I learn from this?"
3. Bible study: stay in the Word, chew on it, swallow it, let it become a part of you.
4. Worship: join a worshipping community when you leave. One Christian is no Christian. You need the support of other believers.
5. Spiritual friends: be careful who you pick to be your friend and when you leave, avoid, if possible, the ones who do you harm or influence you adversely.
6. Don't run from the pain of suffering by escaping into addictions such as TV, shopping, or drugs. We have to have some diversions, but if we get into such activities to avoid pain and refuse to face it, we can block our growth in God.
7. Above all, THANKSGIVING, because God is working a mighty work in your life.

DON'T WASTE YOUR SUFFERING. Given to God, it can bring about immeasurable growth, compassion and love for your salvation and for your ministry to others.

Read: Other Voices

The Stop Signs in Our Lives

Dear God, when life circumstances force me to stop, your Word tells me to wait for You. During these times, I know that it is not You who are hiding from me, but that I'm the one hiding from You. Give me courage to wait when I am blocked from the path I want to walk. Give me the faith to wait until Your Word and my prayers open the way for me to accept your healing for my life in Your time. In the name of the Father, the Son, and the Holy Spirit. Amen.

VOICES FROM THE BIBLE

Read Psalm 25. To know the way of the Lord
For Thee I wait all the day long.

1) Psalm 46 — *Be still and know that I am God*
2) Psalm 40:1-5 — *I waited patiently for the Lord*
3) Genesis 37:5-11, 50:15-21 — *Joseph waited years to see fulfillment*
4) I Samuel 16:6-13 — *David waited before becoming king*
5) James 5:7-11 — *Follow the Old Testament heroes*
6) Phil. 4:4-9 — *What we must do while we wait*

OTHER VOICES

Wait for the Lord. The call is clear. If we are to walk by faith instead of sight, we will have times of waiting. This, too, is God's will. Biblical waiting is not a passive response to decision making; it is faith in action. It is active trust in God and what He is able to provide. As we seek to hear God, there will be times of waiting, and we must resist the temptation to run ahead of Him and His timing.

In every Christian's life there will be times of darkness—times when the way is not clear and the desired light is not immediately forthcoming. When we hit those times, we must trust the Lord and wait on Him. It is a matter of faith to accept that God will give us the light we need when we need it. If we don't have the light we desire, then we must rely on the Lord and wait. The temptation in such circumstance is to produce our own light, but the consequence of such a choice is torment.

Early in Abraham's journey, God revealed His will to Abraham and Sarah. God was going to bless this childless family with a son. Abraham knew God's will, but he did not know how God would accomplish it. When things didn't happen right away, Abraham and Sarah took matters into their own hands. The son they had through striving (Ishmael) only produced strife. He was called "a wild donkey of a man," and throughout the generations his descendants, the Arabs, have strived with Abraham's other descendants, Israel. God still brought forth the promised son, Isaac, but there were consequences to Abraham's self-effort. They learned the hard way that it is not enough to know God's will—we must seek God's will in God's way.

Do you struggle with the temptation to cut corners? In your present situation, do you desire to take shortcuts? Perhaps you sense marriage is in your future, but because of loneliness or longing you are trying to find a mate on your timetable instead of letting God provide one on His. Or maybe you are miserable in your present job, and you realize it is not God's long-term calling for you. Are you waiting for the job God provides, or are you looking for the quickest exit from an undesirable situation?

The biggest threat to waiting is reflected in our unwillingness and in our lack of trust. If I really believe God's will is best, I should be willing to wait for it. Unwillingness to wait is a sign of a deeper problem, likely rooted in a wrong view of God. Remember, His will is always "good and acceptable, and perfect." (Romans 12:2)

YOUR VOICE

1) *Are you patient with God, waiting for His will to be disclosed to you?*
2) *What are you doing as you walk in darkness, waiting for His Light?*
3) *How can being patient make you a better person?*

All above quotes are from *Living God's Will*, Eddie Rasnake, AMG Publishers, Chattanooga, TN. 2001, pp.135-146.

COMMENTARY & DISCUISSION

The Stop Signs in our Lives

Introduction

You are at a stopping place in your life. You've run into a big STOP sign. Sometimes, God makes us wait, puts us on hold. It can be a time of frustration or a time of growth. A former chaplain said that prison/jail can be a "womb of transformation." This is a time of waiting. And when we talk about waiting, we are talking about time.

God's time is different from our time. God's time, expressed by the word *kairos,* means "in the fullness of time," a time when something is ready to happen. A baby (unless a scheduled Caesarean) is born in the fullness of time, when it is ready to come. Flowers bloom in the fullness of time, when they are mature enough to blossom. Our Lord came to the earth in the "fullness of time." One of the reasons may have been that Greek was the common language over much of Africa, Asia and Europe when the Gospel could be spread more easily.

Man's time is measured in clock time: minutes, seconds, and on a larger scale, days, weeks, months, years. The word for our type of time is *chronos*; the word "chronology" comes from this word. We set dates for something and plan for it to happen.

So when we talk about waiting for God, we have to realize that God's answer to prayer, to bringing about the changes we want in our lives, to getting us out of jail, may not be on *chronos* time, on your schedule, but rather on *kairos* time. He may be waiting for something to develop in our lives; more maturity, more patience, more insight into how we need to grow spiritually.

Read Psalm 25

There are three references to "waiting" in this Psalm: "...let none that wait for Thee be put to shame,, "...for Thee I wait all the day long," "...may integrity and uprightness preserve me, for I wait for Thee."

The Psalmist also makes the point that those who wait for God will not be ashamed and that God makes His ways known to him and teaches him His ways. He expresses complete trust in God that only in Him and through His steadfast love will he be cared for and protected. Waiting for that compassionate, loving God will never be in vain.

This man recognizes *kairos*. He is waiting for God to move in his life. What is your response to this Psalm?

1. Psalm 46

What kind of trouble is taking place in vs. 2-4? All kinds of natural calamities and political upheavals are going on. Does that sound like our world today? Storms, floods, tornadoes, political strife, wars, etc. Can we do much about any of this? Who's in charge? The Psalmist in his confidence in God says to come and behold the work of the Lord who ends wars, breaks the weapons. With all this mighty power of God revealed, he then stops and says, "Be still and know that I am God." We ultimately know Him most intimately, not so much through His mighty works and power, but in the silence and quietness of our prayers.

If we slow down, listen, be still and WAIT, will we not recognize that God is in charge and is with us through all of this?

2. Psalm 40:1-5

This is a person who expresses great humility of faith in that he affirms everything that he is and has is a gift from God's hands. This is the "new song" God has put in his mouth, in contrast to the old ways of complaint and despair. This "new song" is a witness to the congregation of God's benevolence and love.

This Psalmist recognizes that while patience is essential, we must also cry out. When we cry out to God, we are putting all of our energy toward seeking Him and His answer to our prayers. And God answers by putting our feet on a rock. And who is this Rock? It is Christ. This security in Christ then frees us up to be a witness to others of God's mercy and compassion.

When have you experienced a deep sense of God's care for you, which prompted you to witness to others?

3. Genesis 37:5-11; 50:15-21

Joseph had to wait a long time before he realized his dreams and even understood them. God had a lot of preparation to do in Joseph's life before he was called to be a member of Pharaoh's court: betrayed by his brothers, sold to the Ishmaelites, serving Potiphar for years, and put in prison for rejecting advances by Potiphar's wife.

However, his brothers also had to wait to receive that forgiveness, wondering for years and experiencing guilt for what they had done to their brother. They may have questioned: Did he escape the Ishmaelites, did he perish in the desert, did he tell the Pharaoh that his family almost murdered him and sold him into slavery? Betrayed him?

They were extremely apprehensive when they discovered Joseph in his high-ranking position and were fearful about how he would receive them. However, as steward to Pharaoh, he was able to meet his brothers and be reconciled with them when they came searching for food. He said to them in chapter 50, "What you intended for evil, God intended for good. I will care for you and your children."

He brought all of his family to Egypt so they would not starve.

Have you had an experience of waiting for a long time for something that helped you and your loved ones? Or a concern about someone who you may have harmed and what their reaction might be to you when you see them again?

4. I Samuel 16:6-13

David had to wait many years and even risk being killed by Saul before he could become king, even though anointed at such a young age. He could have taken a short cut and killed Saul and had many opportunities to do so, but he was a man after God's own heart in spite of the sins of adultery and murder (his deep repentance in Psalm 51 shows his remorse for his sins). Because of these sins, however, he was not allowed to build the Temple for God. That task fell to his son Solomon. David repented of his sins, but he still had to suffer the consequences of those sins.

Do you have trouble repenting for the bad things you have done?

5. James 5:7-11

James warns us to be patient until the Lord comes and not to grumble and complain but be at peace in your circumstances. To wait expectantly and not with anxiety should be our attitude as we wait for God to lead us in the next step of our journey, to open the next door, to remove the next obstacle. Patient acceptance allows God to enter our lives and provide the guidance we need.

The disciples were expecting the Lord's re-appearance to be soon. This coming of the Lord could mean for us His coming into our hearts. The Lord knows that waiting is essential for developing patience, and that is one way He trains us.

Do you have difficulty being patient?

6. Phil. 4:4-9

Have no anxiety about anything, even while we are waiting. Paul tells us to rejoice—we are in the best possible Hands. Christ is in our midst and always will be. And as we wait, we pray and let God know what we need. Paul does not say our prayer will be the answer to what we want, but we will receive the peace that passes all understanding while we wait for God.

And Paul tells us that while we wait we are not to keep our minds on the desperate and dark things of this world but on those things which are good—those things which are honorable, pure, just and gracious. Does this sound like what we see on television or on social media? Be careful where you let your mind rest. We become what we think and what we watch. Children who watch violence on television become more violent. That's why we should keep our minds centered on Christ.

To summarize, here are some of the things we can do in order to grow spiritually while we wait:
1. Stay close to the Lord, listen to his Word, remain faithful through prayer and attend worship as often as possible.
2. Expect good to come as Paul says in Romans 8: "All things work together for good for those who love God and are called according to his purpose."
3. As James says, develop patience, one of the main virtues of the Christian.
4. Lean on Christian friends while you wait. BUT, while we wait, we must remember:
    a. God will keep His promises according to His plan and in His time (*kairos*).
    b. And relating to this, He is never in a hurry. His timing is always perfect. The promises He will keep will be for His glory and for your salvation.

SO, give God glory, not in your successes but even in your brokenness, as Paul did, responding to the Lord's words to him: "My strength is made perfect in weakness." Let others see this witness in you, peacefully accepting what God sends to you.

FNALLY, remember, maybe you are not waiting on God, but rather God may be waiting on you to change: to grow, to pray more, to listen more and, most importantly, to love more.

Read: Other Voices

God, Help Me Get Out of The Pit!

Lord, I am in a pit and calling for Your help in getting out of it. I was either pushed in, I slipped in, or I jumped in. I'm not sure how I got in here, but I need You to lift me up and get me on the right path. I know You hear me when I call, because I'm your beloved child. Please restore to me the joy of my salvation and uphold me with Your everlasting love, and I will praise You forever. In the name of the Father, the Son and the Holy Spirit, Amen.

VOICES FROM THE BIBLE

Read Psalm 40:1-5. A cry for help
I waited patiently for the Lord... He drew me out of the miry pit...

1) Gen 37:12-25   *Joseph is thrown into a pit*
2) Ps. 38:1-8; 18-22   *My foolishness makes me slip into the pit*
3) James 1:13-15   *When I choose evil, I am jumping in the pit*
4) II Cor. 1:8-11   *God delivers us from the pit*
5) Ps. 72:12-14   *God delivers us when we cry out*
6) Ps. 51:1-17   *Create in me a clean heart, O God!*
7) Phil. 3:12-16   *Let go and let God!*

PRAYER HELPS FROM THE BIBLE

Lord God, it is because You love me and keep Your Word that You brought me out with a mighty hand and redeemed me from the land of slavery, from the power of the pharaoh of this world. Help me to absolutely know therefore that You, the Lord my God, are God; You are the faithful God, keeping Your covenant of love to a thousand generations of those who love You and keep Your commands. (Deut. 7:8-9)

As I walk with You, Lord, You will not let my foot slip. You who watch over me will not slumber; indeed, You who watch over Your children will neither slumber nor sleep. You, the Lord, watch over me—You are my shade at my right hand, the sun will not harm me by day nor the moon by night. You, Lord God, will keep me from all harm—You will watch over my life; You will watch over my coming and going both now and forevermore. (Ps. 121:3-8)

Lord God, my Savior, when your kindness and love appeared, You saved me, not because of righteous things I had done, but because of Your mercy. You save me through the washing of rebirth and renewal by the Holy Spirit, whom You poured out on me generously through Jesus Christ my Saviour, so that, having been justified by Your grace, I would become an heir having the hope of eternal life. (Titus 3:4-7)

YOUR VOICE

1) *Have you been pushed in, did you slip in, or did you jump into a pit?*
2) *How are you dealing with it?*
3) *What are some of the obstacles to crying out to God?*
4) *What do you need to confess to get closer to God?*
5) *What do you need to let go?*

Lesson and prayers from *Get Out of that Pit*, Beth Moore, W Publishing Groups, an imprint of Thomas Nelson, Nashville, TN, 2007.

COMMENTARY & DISCUSSION

God, Help Me Get Out of the Pit!

Read 40: 1-5

Jail is not the pit you are in. The Scripture we will be reading refers more to a spiritual, emotional pit which may relate to the one you are in. These are the real pits which dominate our lives and keep us down in the "miry clay" and drive us to addictions of all kinds in order to escape the pain It could be living with an alcoholic, childhood abuse, domestic abuse, emotional scars from such traumas, feelings of hatred, inability to forgive. These types of traumas keep us in the pits that we are looking at today.

Beth Moore, who wrote the book, *Get Out of That Pit*, suffered from sexual abuse as a child as well as alcoholism in her family. She speaks as one who knows. We will follow her outline as she tells how God can help get us out of the pit we are in.

The Psalmist in Psalm 40 refers to the necessity of WAITING on the Lord if we are in a pit. This is a major requirement for getting out of a pit. This is not an emergency room fix, but a long hospital stay which requires that we use the medicine of the church: Bible, prayer, all the means God has given us to help us to heal.

But over time, according to the Psalmist, if we are faithful to God and to our own spiritual growth, God will hear and draw us up from the desolate pit and set our feet on a rock.

What is the ROCK he puts us on? Christ is the rock. And the new song? Praise to God.

Beth Moore mentions three ways that we can end up in a pit. We can be pushed in, we can slip in, or we can jump in. Let's look at examples of each of these and then at three ways we can begin to get out of the pit.

1. Gen. 37:12-25

Joseph was thrown into a pit. His brothers were jealous of him because he was Jacob's favorite son, born of Rachel, his favorite wife. He also had dreams that he shared with his brothers, which depicted them bowing down to him. When Joseph was sent by Jacob to check on the brothers as they were guarding the flock, they wanted to murder him, but Reuben talked them out of that and planned to restore him to Jacob. However, before he could do so, the others sold him to some passing Ishmaelites who were going to Egypt.

How many of you were pushed into a pit?

If we are pushed in due to sexual abuse, domestic violence, being seduced into taking drugs, or some other trauma, a major part of our spiritual work is to forgive. Forgiveness of an early childhood wound is major and has to be done on a daily basis for years. It is like dressing an injury which may finally heal after a long time of tending to it.

Read Genesis 50:15-21

Joseph was moved in his heart to forgive when his brothers came to Egypt to get food during the famine. But Joseph may have been working on forgiveness for a long time, and by the time his brothers came, he was ready to forgive them.

How many of you struggle with forgiving the one who pushed you into a pit?

2. Psalm 38:1-8; 18-22

This writer is admitting that foolishness got him into the pit. He is pleading with God not to get angry with him and acknowledges that he is suffering for what he did.

At first, it is easy to slip into a pit. The high, we figure, is worth the risk. Then the letdown comes, and we suffer physically and in many other ways from this experience.

This Psalmist refers to wounds which foul and fester: his stomach is burning, his whole body aching—is this a hangover from drugs? Also, his heart is suffering, the light has gone from his eyes. It could be physical suffering, or it could be the emotional regret he is experiencing.

In vs. 18, he confesses his wrong. This is the FIRST STEP TO HEALING. In Alcoholics Anonymous meetings, the first step is to recognize your powerlessness over your drinking.

Do you feel you have slipped into a pit? Do these symptoms sound familiar?

3. James 1:13-15

We jump into a pit when we actively choose evil: we hurt someone or break some law or do some sort of intentional evil. Maybe we rob a store to support our drug habit, hurt someone out of rage or retaliation, or molest our children.

James says that desire is at the root of this—the desire for vengeance or money or something else that God does not condone. God does not tempt us. We can't blame God for the results of our sins. Sin has its own consequences.

Did you at one time jump into a pit?

HOW DO WE GET OUT OF THE PIT?

4. II Cor. 1:8-11

God delivers us from the pit, just as he did Paul. Paul experienced a lot of physical disasters in his witness to the faith, but he is proclaiming the fact that God delivered him from them all. But Paul jumped into his own personal pit when he was persecuting Christians, and God had to blind him on the Damascus road. It took a lot to get Paul out of the pit, but God did it, and He can do it for you, too.

Beth Moore says we must:

1) Cry out; let God know we are suffering and turn to Him for help.
2) Confess our wrongdoing if that is what got us into this pit.
3) Consent by letting go and letting God take over.

5. Psalm 72:12-14

We have to acknowledge how needy we are before God can answer us. If we don't cry to him, and resort to some other means to keep from hurting, such as another addiction or some other diversion, we'll never get out. Have you cried out to God either because of your pain of being pushed in, your regret for having slipped in, or the consequences of your jumping in?

6. Ps. 51:1-17

We ask God for three ways to let the Spirit into our hearts, as did David in verses 10, 11, and 12. The Holy Spirit leaves our heart when we sin, and if we jump into a pit as David did when he had Bathsheba's husband killed in order to commit adultery, we have to do major repentance. Psalm 51 is the classic Psalm of repentance. This is what begins the healing process. This is the Psalm David wrote in repentance for murder and adultery.

Is repentance difficult for you as you remember jumping into a pit?

7. Phil 3:12-16

Paul sanctioned the death of Stephen, the first martyr of the church. Acts says he was ravaging the church, entering house after house to drag off Christian men and committing them to prison. Paul had a lot to let go and leave behind, yet he "pressed on to the goal for the prize of the upward call of God in Christ Jesus." Because he focused on Christ, rather than his own past sins, he was able to move on in his journey to Christ.

What are some of the things we have to let go? The past, control of others, fears, hate, lack of forgiveness, others?

Read Psalm 40 again.

Then read: Prayer Helps from the Bible

Dear God, Please Help Me Deal with the Missing Pieces in My Life

God, You know we all have missing pieces in our lives, whether it be wounds from abuse, a broken marriage, lost children, bad health, or other afflictions. These missing pieces can drive us to do bad things to ourselves just to deal with the pain. We run into worse trouble when we attempt to fill up those holes ourselves without turning to You for help. You came to earth to seek us out, those of us who are running in every direction except into Your arms. Help us to throw our lives into reverse. Help us to look to You as our only, best and most sublime hope, knowing that You can help us deal with our losses and our lack and fill them with the love and joy that comes from surrender to You. In the name of the Father, the Son and the Holy Spirit. Amen.

VOICES FROM THE BIBLE

Read Psalm 116. The Lord hears our supplications.
Because he inclined his ear to me, therefore I will call on him as long as I live.

1) Romans 8:31-39 — *Does God Care?*
2) Matt. 20:1-7 — *Is God Fair?*
3) Luke 24:13-35 — *Is God There?*
4) Psalm 139 — *God are You Aware?*
5) Matt. 7:7-11 — *God, do You Hear Prayer?*

OTHER VOICES

Every missing piece is a snapshot. What you struggle with—whether it's debt, disease, or any number of difficulties—is not the whole picture. It's just one photo in the whole photo album that is your life. It is not forever; it really will pass away some day. Just like an old photo in an album, the pain will become a faded memory. Keep your missing piece in perspective—eternal perspective. II Corinthians 4: 16-18 will remind you that your missing piece is temporary.

Every missing piece is a picture. Your struggles may cause you to experience loss, but you can also gain wisdom and deeper understanding as you allow them to teach you. Think about what knowledge you have found in your missing piece. What foolishness have you left behind because of what you learned from it? Read Psalms 25:3, 86:11; Roman 5:3 when you need encouragement in the classroom of suffering.

Every missing piece is a ministry. Your missing pieces can be opportunities to redeem your loss and give to others. For example, the apostle Paul wrote the books of Colossians, Philemon, Ephesians and Philippians while he was in prison in Rome. He could have seen that prison—that missing piece—as an opportunity for self-pity or ministry hiatus. Paul could have spent his time in prison asking, "Why God?" He could have stared at the shackles he wore and cried out, "God, are you fair? God, are you aware of me in this prison?"

Some people spend their whole lives asking questions of faith like, "God, do You hear prayer? God, are You there? God, do You care?" But what if you take those same kinds of questions and ask, "Do I care? Am I there for others? Am I aware of the world around me? Am I an answer to the prayers of others?" When we become part of the answer for others who suffer, the questions concerning our own suffering seems to move to a place of less significance.

YOUR VOICE

Consider these questions and ask how your missing pieces can allow you to minister to others.

Lesson and Other Voices based on *Missing Pieces: Real Hope when Life Doesn't Make Sense*, Jennifer Rothschild, LifeWay Press, Nashville, TN, 37234-0152 2012.

COMMENTARY & DISCUSSION

Dear God, Please Help me Deal with the Missing Pieces in My Life

Introduction

Everyone has missing pieces in their lives. These missing pieces can be broken relationships, drug addiction, severe illness, and/or childhood abuse. And even a bitter and negative outlook can reflect unaddressed missing pieces. The good news of the Gospel is that Christ can fill in those missing pieces and restore us to wholeness. With His loving power, our faithful diligence and attention to our healing, we can become what we are called to become in Him. "I come to make all things new." Rev. 21:5.

Only God knows why we are suffering, why there are missing pieces in our lives, and only God can ultimately provide the cure.

What is one missing piece in your life?

Read Psalm 116

This is a man who has been gloriously restored, who has come near death and been brought back by God who has "dealt bountifully with him."

He acknowledges that he kept the faith though he was greatly afflicted. Maybe he had many missing pieces.

He ends the Psalm by wondering how he can repay God. He affirms that it is through joining the congregation in worship that he can show his gratitude by offering thanksgiving to God.

This must be our response when God restores the "missing pieces" in our lives. We not only give thanks, but we worship in community with others.

Do you see this as an appropriate response when God has helped to make you whole?

1. Romans 8:31-39: *God, do you care?*

God's love is the unshakeable foundation of the Christian life.

The apostle Paul names the stark forces in his day that beset people: tribulation, famine, nakedness, peril or sword. Our trials today, also, can be physical threats, but more often they are internal sins and weaknesses which bring us down: our own failures, spiritual vacuums and despair, failure of others to support us, and life circumstances such as poverty, health needs, homelessness, and jail time. However, we must believe and exclaim as Paul does that "nothing can separate us from the love of God." That's what holds us together as we address these missing pieces. Believing in this Power can make things right or enable us to endure, secure in His love.

With such overwhelming love, God is going to do everything to help us to deal with the missing pieces. He will take on our pain and bear it with us.

How can we let go and let God fill in those holes in our lives? It is a matter of surrendering and opening up your heart to God, trusting that He will bring good out of any negative circumstance. Just see yourself a passenger in the car that God is driving.

When tragedy strikes, do you first think of how much God loves you and will see you through it and help you make something good of it?

2. Matt. 20:1-7: *Is God fair?*

In this parable, is the householder fair? He gave the same wages to the laborers who worked one hour as he did to those who worked all day. The laborers who worked all day received what they agreed on. They only grumbled when they saw the one-hour laborers get the same.

God doesn't grade on the curve. In other words, He gives each of us what He believes is best for us to grow spiritually. We may look at others who have not suffered as much, who have all the good things of life and yet do not seem to be serving the Lord as devoutly as we are, and we become jealous.

Yet the Lord says, in this parable, that He will decide how much to reward each of us and will provide for us in the best way for our own salvation.

God is fair, but not in the ways of the world.

The last line of that parable sums it up: the first shall be last and the last shall be first. Jesus is referring to the Jews who had been given the Covenant and who God had guided through the centuries with the Law and His special care, but they did not recognize the true Messiah and so rejected Christ. Whereas those of the New Covenant, Christian Gentiles who responded to Christ, will be first in the Kingdom, and many of the Jews may be last.

In what ways has God been fair to you? Has He given you what you need to work on healing the missing pieces?

3. Luke 24:13-35: *Is God there?*

This is one of the most beautiful of the post-resurrection stories. The two disciples/apostles are walking toward Emmaus and discussing the recent events which occurred in Jerusalem, when a Stranger joins them and asks what they are talking about. They share the news of Jesus' death and disappearance. The Stranger then goes through all the Old Testament Scriptures to show them that the Messiah had to suffer and die before being received in Glory. They are entranced by His words and later remark about how their hearts burned within them as He talked. When they get near to their destination, they invite Him to join them for supper, and as He blesses and breaks the bread, their eyes are opened. They recognize Him as the Lord, and He disappears.

The two disciples later shared this event with the other disciples and claimed they did not know who He was until the breaking of the bread.

The "breaking of the bread", the Eucharist (some churches today refer to this as "communion"), was central in the early church, and Luke is emphasizing this reality in this account.

But apart from that, have you experienced an especially meaningful moment or encounter with a holy friend, a beautiful sunset, or a moving piece of writing, and when you look back, you knew God was there speaking to you? That He was there all along loving and hovering over you?

Has this happened to you? Do you think that may have been God in disguise?

4. Psalm 139: *God, are you aware?*

The Psalmist strongly affirms in this particular psalm that God knows everything about us, that He was there when we were in the womb, and He knows when our life will end. Further, He knows whether we are lying down or getting up, He is familiar with all of our plans, not a word from our mouth does He not know, and He guards us and spreads His hand over us.

No one, not the most intimate member of our families—mother, father, spouse, children—knows us like God knows us.

He also knows all those missing pieces in our lives and yearns to love us into wholeness. So how do we respond to that all-knowing, all-loving, all-aware God? We love Him back. This is not easy to do with all the false and crazy "loves" competing for our attention in this sin-ridden world. We must become single-minded through lots of prayer, Bible study, worship and attention to our lifestyle. We must be circumspect and careful in where we devote our time, our energies, and our thoughts. Being in jail can give you some "time out" from the world and be a "womb of transformation" for you. Don't waste this opportunity for spiritual growth.

And then we will be so attuned to God's care, we can say with the Psalmist as he ends his plea to God, "Watch me lest I follow any path that grieves Thee and guide me in the way everlasting."

What are some of the ways you choose to open yourself up to God's love?

5. Matt 7:7-11: *God, do you hear prayer?*

We have to ask, seek, knock, and trust that if we ask for bread and fish, He won't give us stones and serpents. In other words, if we ask for our daily spiritual and physical needs, He will supply them.

Does God hear, and, if so, why doesn't He give us what we pray for? He may answer by giving us something more beneficial than what we are praying for, e.g. patience in waiting, a greater intimacy with Him, a change of our perspective or priorities. And even if we are praying for reconciliation with someone, God may put that on hold until that person grows closer to God.

Jesus is our model for prayer. Jesus experienced unanswered prayer in the Garden of Gethsemane. He asked in His agony, "Let this cup pass from Me, yet not My will but Thine be done." God refused to let it pass.

God answered it in an incredibly different way, in order to bring about our salvation through His Son's death and resurrection.

So finally, we must surrender to the God who is in charge of our lives and trust that God will answer our prayer when perhaps these conditions are met:

- In His time, when I am ready.
- When I've learned what I needed to learn.
- When I can love God enough to trust Him with the answer He chooses to give me.

Wait on the Lord. His silence doesn't mean He's not working for you. He is simply enabling you to deepen your trust in Him.

Read: Other Voices

God, When the Storms of Life Assail Me, Help Me to Trust in You

Dear God, when the stormy sea of life threatens to take me under, help me to know that You Who walk on water are in control and that Your nail-scarred hand is reaching out to me to rescue me from the stormy and threatening deep. You parted the waters of the Red Sea and the waters of the Jordan to let Your people pass through, and I know You will calm the waters that threaten to take me under and will keep me safe and secure. Help me to have that faith in You. In the name of the Father, the Son and the Holy Spirit. Amen

VOICES FROM THE BIBLE

Read Job 38:4-11; 42:2-6. Our God is an awesome God.
Who shut the sea with doors, when it burst forth from the womb?

1. Ps. 107:23-31   *The peril of the storm*
2. Matt. 14:22-33   *The prayer of the storm*
3. Matt 8:23-27   *Peace in the storm*
4. Heb. 12:3-13   *The purpose of the storm*
5. Ps. 102:32-43   *Praise after the storm*

OTHER VOICES

Sometimes in the face of trouble, we foolishly ask, "Why me?" when it might be more appropriate to ask, "Why not me?" We suffer because we are human. Jesus declared that a blind man's inability to see was not caused by his sin or his parents' sin but was an opportunity for God's power to be revealed (John 9: 1-4). Viewing our trials as punishments by an angry God is not likely to help us cope. Our trials may, however, contain lessons we need to learn, and suffering often helps us grow spiritually (Romans 5:3-4). We can open ourselves to this possibility by asking, "What does God want me to learn in this situation?"
-Jane P. Ives

We are members of the Body of Christ. This is our most basic identity, and it defines our most basic calling (Rom. 12; I Cor. 12). "If one member suffers," St. Paul affirms, "all suffer together" (I Cor 12:25). Yet the Head of the Body suffers as well. This means that whatever we experience is never experienced in isolation. We never suffer alone. Although other members of the Body may be oblivious to our suffering, Christ bears it to the full. We know that He even longs to assume our suffering to assimilate it to His own, in order to transfigure it and ourselves into the image of His wholeness and His ineffable peace. This is the great truth of the Cross: that Jesus freely and lovingly unites Himself with us, not only to redeem us from sin and guilt, but to share our suffering and to bear it to the end.
-John Breck

Then I saw a new heaven and a new earth; for the first heaven and the first earth had passed away, and the sea was no more. And I saw the holy city, new Jerusalem, coming down out of heaven from God, prepared as a bride adorned for her husband, and I heard a loud voice from the throne saying, "Behold, the dwelling of God is with men. He will dwell with them, and they shall be his people, and God himself will be with them; he will wipe away every tear from their eyes, and death shall be no more, neither shall there be mourning nor crying nor pain any more, for the former things have passed away." And He who sat upon the throne said, "Behold, I make all things new." Also, he said, "Write this, for these words are trustworthy and true."
-Revelation 21:1-5

YOUR VOICE

1. *What inner storm are you experiencing now?*
2. *What resources are you using to deal with it?*
3. *Is there a special Scripture passage that is helpful?*
4. *Do you think God is in the storm with you?*

This lesson is taken, in part, from *When Your World Falls Apart,* David Jeremiah, W Publishing Group, Nashville, TN, 37014, 2000.

COMMENTARY & DISCUSSION

God, When the Storms of Life Assail Me, Help Me to trust in You

Read Job 38:4-11, 42:2-6

These passages affirm the fact that God is beyond our understanding. We can't begin to fully know how He created the earth, why He created it, and for what purpose. What we do know for certain, by looking at Christ, is that God is love, and through that love God created the world and created us to love Him.

But some people seek knowledge above love because it is far easier to learn facts than it is to love. However, if religion is just an intellectual effort, it can cause all sorts of dissents. "Knowledge puffs up, love builds up," Paul says. "The head without the heart is nothing", says Chaim Potok in his book *The Chosen*.

Job finally realizes this when he says to God, "Now I see Thee." God has revealed his love to Job, who repents (that word literally means "melts") in God's presence and has no more questions. God knew that Job didn't need to know why, he only needed to know the Who—the God of love who created him.

It is love, that all powerful, intimate love of God, that gets us through the storm. We do not need an explanation of why we are suffering—what good would it do to know why?—we only need to know the crucified One who hung on the Cross out of love for us.

Christianity is about a relationship, not about a lot of knowledge. God didn't call us to be right so much as righteous—loving toward Him and others.

1. Ps. 107:23-31

What are the perils we face today? If we look out at our world, the perils are numerous: climate change, political unrest, unending wars, corruption at every level of government, an unending array of disasters. But more important are the perils we face in our own lives: troubled or abusive relationships, domestic violence. abuse of children, addiction, disease, poverty.

We can become paralyzed by the perils. We can walk around so frightened and fearful that we resort to escapes in all forms; addictions to anything from shopping to drugs are attempts to use our own man-made mechanisms to escape our fear, doubt, and worry.

But what did those sailors in the Psalms do? They stopped looking at the raging sea and looked up, and they cried to the Lord. He heard their prayer and calmed the sea.

That also must be our answer to the perils we face. We must look up and cry to the Lord and trust that He will send the calm that we need in our lives and hearts.

Are you paralyzed by the perils? What are you doing about it? What resources has God given to you to help you deal with them?

2. Matt. 14:22-33

Peter tried to do something he could only do by focusing on Christ, because when he began looking at the stormy waves, he sank. He attempted to do the impossible without the focus on the Power that could support him. When he cried out for help, Jesus reached out his hand and rescued him saying, "O man of little faith, why did you doubt?"

The focus on this text is the "prayer" of the storm. What was Peter's prayer as he began to sink? What did he say when he cried out to the Lord? He said, "Lord, save me!" From earliest Christian times, the faithful would use brief prayers, repeated over and over, to get closer to God. One of the ones that has lasted through the ages is called "The Jesus Prayer." The words are, "Lord Jesus Christ, Son of God, have mercy on me." The practice of this prayer on a daily basis, said over and over, is said to open your heart to God, calm your soul, and bring you closer to Him.

The word "mercy" is the translation of the Hebrew word "hesed," which means "steadfast love." So when you pray the Jesus Prayer, you are actually saying, "Lord Jesus Christ, Son of God, put your steadfast love into my heart."

This could be an especially effective way of dealing with the storms in your life, when you are about to sink into a raging sea.

Have you ever tried to do something nearly impossible without God? What happened?

3. Matt. 8: 23-27

This is another incident of the disciples in a boat on a stormy sea. Jesus is in the boat with them, but asleep. The storm begins raging, and again the disciples panic and shout, "Save us, Lord, we are perishing!" Again, he accuses them of having little faith. But did He go back to sleep and let them struggle? No, He rebuked the wind and the sea, and there was great calm.

He went to the source of their fear and calmed the sea; He addressed the source of their problem and solved it.

Do you sometimes believe that God is asleep? You pray and plead and beg, but there is no answer. You give up, thinking He has forgotten you. You mistakenly turn to other solutions or comforts, but at some point, when all else fails, you realize that God is right there with you, protecting, hovering, saving you.

Sometimes we don't recognize the way is which God is with us and protecting us. Your time in jail may be a protection against something far more evil.

But even in jail, you can experience a sustaining peace. Paul tells us the conditions for that in Philippians 4:6-7: "'Have no anxiety about anything, but in everything by prayer and supplication, with thanksgiving, let your requests be made known to God. And the peace of God, which passes all understanding, will keep your hearts and your minds in Christ Jesus."

It is through prayer, supplication and thanksgiving that the peace of God which passes all understanding will keep us. Again, this is not just an intellectual promise that all will go well, but one delivered into our hearts to give us the deep confidence that God is with us.

After the sea was calmed by the Lord, the disciples marveled about what type of Man this must be, when even the winds and the sea obey Him. This was the awe that came over them at witnessing such Power. We, too, must be in awe of such a God who delivers us so often in so many ways.

What is your most recent experience of God calming the sea in your life?

4. Heb. 12:3-13

The book of Hebrews was written for Jewish Christians who may have been going through persecution, but more certainly, they were having their faith severely tested. Therefore, the writer is urging them to remain faithful. He says that the struggle they are going through is because God is intending to strengthen them, and the suffering they are experiencing is to discipline them, even as earthly fathers discipline their children.

God disciplines us for our own good, Hebrews says, so that we may share in His holiness and receive the "peaceful fruit of righteousness." They are admonished to "lift up your drooping hands and strengthen your weak knees." In modern lingo, "Get a grip and hang in there!"

So the purpose of the storm is to bring you closer to God and to your salvation through the experience of your suffering.

Can you see that what you are going through in your jail experience might be a type of training and purification, forcing you to focus on God to help you grow into His likeness?

Share.

5. Ps. 107: 32-43

Praise should always follow deliverance from the storm. Maybe that's why God allows the storms in our lives, to provoke praise from us. When our lives are going well with no immediate problems facing us, we forget to praise God for what we do have. Sometimes it takes hard times, struggles, disappointments, and failures to force us to turn to God and become more grateful for our blessings.

God may send the storms to get our attention, as He wants to be in communion with us to a degree we could not possibly imagine. It is through being in constant communion with God through the tools He has given us—prayer, Bible study, worship, and most of all praise—that we become most like Him. And therein lies our salvation—to become like God.

Read: Other Voices

COMFORT

Lord, When I Carry Heavy Burdens, I Need Your Comfort

Sometimes, Lord, what I really need is comfort. I know I have made bad choices and am suffering the consequences, but I also know that Your mercy is far greater than Your judgment. You also have said in your Word that you are willing to leave the ninety-nine sheep to go after the lost one, to bring that lost one back to the fold to be loved and cared for. Please bring this lost sheep back so I can be restored to Your care and to the comfort only You can give. In the name of the Father, the Son and the Holy Spirit. Amen

VOICES FROM THE BIBLE

Read Psalm 107:1-3; 10-16. The Lord rescues us.
He delivered them from their distress; he brought them out of darkness and gloom.

1. Psalm 23 — *The Lord shepherds me*
2. Matt. 11:25-30 — *His yoke is easy and His burden is light*
3. John 14:1-7 — *Let not your hearts be troubled*
4. II Cor.12: 1-10 — *Sometimes we are refused comfort*
5. II Cor.l :3-7 — *We are comforted in order to comfort others*
6. Rom. 8:28-38 — *The ultimate comfort: how much God loves us*

OTHER VOICES

When I live in the awareness of God's presence all around me, I am an open person, an open individual, living life open to His scrutiny. He is conscious of every circumstance I encounter. He attends me with care and concern because I belong to Him. And this will continue through eternity. What an assurance! I shall dwell in the presence (in the care of) the Lord forever. Bless His Name!
-Phillip Keller

I've known physical pain sometimes; other times, guilt or grief; still other times, emotional hurts, lurking memories, worry over others, anxiety about the future. Pain, nonetheless. And yet, dear loving Lord, you've helped me discover a liberating truth: When the storm clouds bring me to a realization of how much I need You and I cry out to You and thank You for reaching across my imagined breach of separation from you, You assure me of Your love and help me make a fresh start. Then I hear You say, "I will never forget you; I remember my covenant; you belong to Me."
-Lloyd John Ogilvie

If evil at its overwhelming worst has already been met and mastered, as in Jesus Christ it has; if God has got his hands on this baffling mystery of suffering in its direct, more defiant form, and turned its most awful triumph into uttermost, irrevocable defeat; if that in fact has happened, and on that scale, are you to say it cannot happen on the infinitely lesser scale of our own union with Christ through faith? In heart-breaking things that happen to us, those mental agonies, those spiritual midnights of the soul, we are "more than conquerors," not through our own valor or stoic resolution, not through

a creed or code of philosophy, but "through Him who loved us"—through the thrust and pressure of the invading grace of Christ.
-James S. Stewart

When we draw near to God, He is always ready to welcome us with outstretched arms. He will pour out His mercy and comfort and give us His enabling strength and power to walk through whatever happens in our lives. When pain, suffering, persecution, and trials come, what will you do? Will you trust in yourself and what you can do? Or will you trust in the One who is able to do exceedingly, abundantly above what you could ask or think? When you seem to have no strength of your own, that's when you can most fully rest in the One whose strength is made perfect in your weakness.
-Kay Arthur

YOUR VOICE

1. *How can I more fully open myself to the Lord's comfort?*
2. *Who on earth can I lean on in these dark times of pain and regret?*
3. *Am I willing to take on the easy yoke and light burden of the Lord by trusting Him in all things?*
4. *What can I do to stay closer to the Good Shepherd's fold so I won't be tempted to wander off into the wilderness?*

COMMENTARY & DISCUSSION

Lord, When I Carry Heavy Burdens, I Need Your Comfort

Read Psalm 107: 1-3, 10-16

What impresses you about this Psalm?

Our comfort comes through knowing that when we cry out to God, He will deliver us, not necessarily on our timeline, nor in the specific way we choose, but He always hears us and attends to our needs according to His will.

1. Psalm 23

This is a familiar Psalm to all. What does it mean to you?

Christ is our shepherd. In John 10, the Lord assures us that He is the Good Shepherd and will lay down His life for his sheep. The Lord goes after the lost sheep, even if He has to leave the ninety-nine, because one sheep will die if separated from the flock. The sheep hear His voice and will move toward Him, but if they hear the voice of a stranger, they will move away.

The Psalmist says that the Shepherd will provide what we need: He leads us beside still waters. This could mean He quiets our soul, provides stillness in our lives so that we can hear Him.

- He uses a rod to keep away our enemies
- He uses his staff for guidance, to steer us into the right path.
- The table He prepares for us could be seen today as the Lord's Supper at our church.
- We don't fear death because He has conquered death by His death and Resurrection.

He is near to us, and because of that we can say with the Psalmist, "Surely goodness and mercy shall follow me all the days of my life, and I will dwell in the house of the Lord forever."

Have you experienced an occasion when this Psalm was particularly meaningful to you?

2. Matt 11:25-30

It is not necessarily the learned, the educated, or even the theologian who is open to receive the truth. Jesus was probably referring to the Pharisees and Scribes who knew and kept the law but criticized Jesus because He broke the law by expressing love as He did when He healed on the Sabbath.

Rather, it is the innocent, those who are open, humble, and childlike who more likely can receive the good news.

In this passage, the Lord provides the assurance that to walk in His way promises comfort and release from our world-weary burdens. If we come to Him, we will find that His yoke is easy (it is still a yoke) and His burden is light (it is still a burden).

What is His yoke? It was the law to the Jews which indeed was a yoke and a burden, because no one could fulfill all the many laws which had accumulated by the time Jesus came. For Jesus it was the yoke of love, the commandment to love God and neighbor. When we can truly love, all life becomes joy and our yoke becomes easy.

Our burden is our cross, and our cross is the trials, hardships, and sufferings which come to us in our lives. "Take up your cross and follow me," says our Lord. Our cross (burden) only becomes "light" when we follow and keep our eyes on Christ. If we try to carry our cross without looking to Him and leaning on Him, it will become so heavy that it will become impossible for us to bear.

How does that apply to your being here in jail? Can you take on the "yoke" of love toward God and others, and can you look to Christ as you carry the "burden" of your cross?

3. John 14:1-7

This is our Lord's final discourse to his disciples in which He tells them that He will leave them. He assures the disciples that He comes from God, so to have faith in God is to have faith in Him. He tells them that there are many dwellings which await them. He also tells them that He has to leave so that the Comforter will come.

When the disciples ask where he is going and how can they know the way, He answers that He is the Way, the Truth and the Life. And what is the "way" where He is going?

His crucifixion, death, and resurrection for our salvation is the Way; the Truth is His person because He comes from God and is the second person of the Trinity; He is the Life given to us so that we may have eternal life in Him and His abundant life within us on earth.

What is a greater comfort than to be aware of all our Lord offers?

4. Cor. 12:1-10

Paul refers to his vision in the 3rd person. He does not want to boast that he had a mystical experience, which he describes as being caught up in the third heaven. So that he would not be too elated about this experience, the Lord sent him a "thorn in the flesh." Most scholars agree that this was some sort of chronic, physical problem that was weighing him down. Paul asked the Lord three times to remove it, but the Lord refused to take it away. He saw that Paul would be forced to lean on Him more fully if this weakness was allowed to remain. Paul accepted this and takes pleasure in his suffering, because when he is weak (not able to rely on his own strength and resources) he is strong (in Christ).

Paul then realized that the promise of the continuation of Christ's grace was all that was needed for him and that "when I am weak, then I am strong."

If we trust in Christ, then the weaker we are, the more the Divine Power can work in us.

You may feel your weakest and most vulnerable here in jail, and it is here that God may be working most profoundly in you. What God can do through your weakness is far beyond what you can do in your strength.

Have you experienced that in any way in your life, especially since you have been here?

5. II Cor. 1:3-7

Those who have suffered certain trials and have dealt with them through Christ are better equipped to comfort those who may be suffering in the same way. Henri Nouwen, a priest in Canada who ministered to people with disabilities, wrote a book entitled *The Wounded Healer*, in which he discusses this. Apparently, his own difficulties and challenges with depression and other negative issues enabled him to be an effective helper to those with similar problems. The leaders in AA and NA groups who have conquered alcoholism or drugs oftentimes speak with much greater authority than those who have not had that experience.

Do you feel that some of the trials you have experienced have strengthened you and that this enables you to help others going through similar experiences?

6. Romans 8:28-38

All things work together for good for those who love God. You have to love God for all things to work together for good. This certainly is a major comfort for those of us who struggle to love God.

God does not force His will on us. He knows who will choose, out of their free will, to follow Him. He didn't force you to come to Bible study, just as He didn't restrain those who didn't come. Because you came and want to know Him better, if that's why you're here, you are in the process of being conformed to the image of His Son. Those He predestined, called, and justified are those He foresaw would choose him. Nothing can separate us from this God of love we have chosen to accept and to follow.

This love of God is the unshakeable foundation of the Christian life, and it is our ultimate and most profound comfort. This comfort quite often comes to us through others.

Have you experienced God's loving comfort and been able to offer it to others? Has the comfort offered you by someone made a difference in your life?

Read: Other Voices

Dear God, Send Your Peace into My Troubled Heart

Dear Prince of Peace, who gives peace beyond what the world gives, I need Your peace today. The stresses and strains of this place, and of my own weary soul, rob me of the peace I need to survive. I know Your peace is the healing balm that can get me through. But I know that it can only come from trusting You in all things. Please enable me to have that trust and completely surrender into Your care. In the name of the Father, the Son and the Holy Spirit.

VOICES FROM THE BIBLE

Read Psalm 4. The peace from on high
In peace I will both lie down and sleep.

1) John 14:25-31   *A peace not of this world*
2) Gal. 5:22-26   *One fruit of the Spirit is peace*
3) Phil. 4:4-13   *Thou doest keep him in perfect peace*
4) Luke 12:49-53   *Not peace, but a sword!*
5) Mark 4:35-41   *"Peace, be still" to the waves and the wind*

OTHER VOICES

The fact that Jesus admonishes us to not allow our hearts to be troubled or fearful is an acknowledgement that there is a choice involved... We are not to give in to the temptations to be troubled or fearful when circumstances do not go the way we desire. In a nutshell, God's peace is the absence of a troubled heart. Like a diamond displayed on black velvet, it is most clearly seen when contrasted to difficult circumstances.
-Eddie Rasnake

Finding the peace of the Lord within requires taking time to be truly and completely still. This means that you open your ears and heart only to the Lord, shutting out all distractions, including those of your own petitions and desires. In fact, your only desire to seeking peace should be to hear the Lord's voice—in Scripture and in your heart. This might seem like an impossible task. But Jesus, awaiting his arrest and crucifixion, sets the example. "Thy will be done."
-Maureen Platt

A man cannot create peace in his own soul. It is not packaged with great intellect, talent or sensitivity. By six years of age, Wolfgang Amadeus Mozart, the Austrian composer of the 1700s, was an accomplished musician on the clavier, violin, and organ and the composer of five works frequently performed today. By the age of 14, he was commissioned to write his first serious opera, establishing what was already a phenomenal profession. Rarely has one life held such promise; rarely has one future been more secure. But Mozart was wracked by an inner turmoil that not only stole from him length of days, but also the quality of those same days. He died a pauper at the age of 34 and was buried in an unmarked grave, surrounded by only a handful of friends. He never discovered what he

continually searched for between the notes of a page: peace. He was only one of millions who are much less famous and have never captured that which makes life bearable.
-Beth Moore

Lord, make me an instrument of your peace. Where there is hatred, let me sow love; where there is injury, pardon; where there is doubt, faith; where there is despair, hope; where there is darkness, light. O dear Master, grant that I may not so much seek to be consoled as to console; to be understood as to understand; to be loved as to love. For it is in giving that we receive, it is in pardoning that we are pardoned, and it is by dying that we are born to eternal life. Amen
-St. Francis

YOUR VOICE

1) *What thoughts give me the most peace?*
2) *What circumstances give me the most peace? (Where you are, who you are with, what you are doing, etc.)*
3) *What has been your experience of finding true peace in your life, even in the midst of turmoil?*
4) *What are some of the obstacles you have encountered to finding such peace? What strategies were most helpful?*
5) *Is it possible to find perfect peace?*

COMMENTARY & DISCUSSION

Dear God, Send Your Peace into My Troubled Heart

Introduction

The "Prince of Peace" was born into a world fragmented, from His day to ours, with violence, wars, conflict, hatred, and turmoil. The message of peace which He brought to us was in such opposition to the ways of the world that we killed Him. And yet His message, "Peace be with you" was the one with which He greeted His followers at every encounter with them after the Resurrection. And even today, at some time during worship services at most Christian churches, these same words are said to the flock.

So what does "peace" mean today in our tormented world? It can only mean that true peace must come from above. A saint once observed that "The person of peace will bring thousands around him to peace." Why? They radiate a serenity which comes from above—not from the world but from the Holy Spirit.

Let's talk about the "peace of the world" vs. "peace from above" as we look at Scriptures.

Read Psalm 4

This is a prayer of confidence, of a man who rejoices in his faith and confronts those who are disheartened. He maintains that a heart which fears (is in awe of) God and trusts in God is all that matters.

Why do fear/awe and trust go together? Because fear/awe of God recognizes that He is all powerful, all loving, and in control of the final outcome of our lives. For this very reason, we can put our ultimate trust in Him.

Thus the Psalmist promises us that we can lie down in peace and sleep because this God can make us dwell in safety.

How difficult is this for you to have both awe of God and trust in Him?

1. John 14:15-31

This is the farewell talk by Jesus to His disciples. He has warned them that He will be crucified but is providing assurance that when He goes away, He will come again (the Resurrection).

He promises He will send a Comforter to care for them while He is gone (after the Ascension). This Comforter will teach them and keep before them all that He had said.

This Comforter is the Holy Spirit. How often do you call on the Holy Spirit for comfort?

Then Jesus goes on to offer them His peace, not as the world gives. This peace belongs to Christ and is only His to give to us. We receive it by having confident trust in God, belief in His love and surrender to His will.

What type of peace does the world give? It is circumstantial; i.e., when all is going well for you: happy marriage, happy children, enough money, and a good job. These are what give you the world's peace. But how long do those conditions last? What happens when they are taken away? The world's peace is temporary, distorted, and unsatisfactory. When it is taken away, we can be left bereft and turn to many false avenues to peace, such as addictions ranging from shopping to drugs.

Our culture is built on false promises of peace because that is what sells products. How do you deal with finding peace? Where do you look?

2. Gal. 5:22-26

Peace is given to us as one of the fruits of the Spirit. This is God's peace that comes to us when we draw close to Him and invoke the Holy Spirit into our lives. These fruits are love, joy, peace, patience, kindness, goodness, faithfulness, gentleness and self-control.

When the Holy Spirit comes into our lives, we will experience all the gifts of the Spirit. When we have one, we will have them all in varying degrees. One gift may be stronger in you than the others, while other people may experience different degrees of other fruits. But since peace is one of the fruits, we can see that receiving the gifts of the Holy Spirit is the way to gain peace.

A life of prayer, Bible Study, and worship will enable us to receive and manifest the fruits of the Spirit. As Paul says, not only does the Spirit keep us in Christ, but we also walk by the Spirit, and that means manifesting the fruits to others, especially that of peace.

Someone said, "In His will is our peace," and St. Augustine said, "Our hearts are restless until they rest in Thee."

What type of peace are you experiencing these days? Can you be at peace while in jail?

3. Phil. 4:4-13

Suffering is inevitable, anxiety is optional. We have a choice as to whether or not to be anxious. Some people, however, have a chemical or hormone imbalance which can make them overanxious. However, there is medication for this condition that a person can choose to take. So all of us have a choice as to whether or not to be anxious.

Paul admonishes us to "Let your requests be known to God." There is no guarantee they will be filled according to our wishes, but the promise is that He will send His peace. This is not a peace based on how things are going in your life. It will be a peace from above that will keep your hearts and minds in Christ.

This can be a peace beyond understanding. For instance, you are in jail. Can you have peace in here while not knowing your future? If that is peace in Christ, then that is beyond understanding, not related to your circumstances, but due to your faith in Christ.

There are conditions, however, for receiving this peace: prayer, supplications (requests), and always thanksgiving. Further, Bible study and worship add to your receptivity to this peace.

Another mandate from Paul is to think on holy things. If you dwell on the violence and craziness of this world that comes to us through all the various media and daily news, you will become very negative in your thinking, a sure block to inner peace. We become like what we focus on, where our minds dwell. Paul says to think about things that are honorable, pure, lovely, gracious, excellent, and worthy of praise. Meditate on these things and follow the traditions of the Church, then you will receive God's peace.

The good things we can think on are not limited to the Bible, but we have to be careful and discerning. There is some good on television, great literature, beautiful art and gorgeous sunsets to look at. Think of your children and/or grandchildren. A Russian writer, Dostoevsky, wrote in one of his novels that if you have just one good memory from childhood, that will supply much comfort and peace in later life. Just be careful what you ponder on. Sometimes just being silent—the language of God—can be the way to perfect peace.

Paul was content (at peace) in whatever circumstances he found himself. Changing circumstances did not bother him, as he was grounded in Christ. Someone once said, "When all I had left was God, I realized that God was all I needed." That's Paul, the Apostle!

Where is your mind most of the time?

4. Luke 12:49-53

The word "hate" is translated as "divided' in most versions of the Bible. Why does Jesus talk about bringing a sword and not peace?

Jesus means a spiritual sword which will divide those who speak the truth from those who do not. And these divisions can occur within families. How many of you agree totally with other family member regarding some spiritual truth? How many of you have tried to insist on doing the right thing and believing the right beliefs and have been criticized and not supported by family members?

That is what Jesus means: the sword of truth will divide even the most intimate relationships. There can be no peace unless all are in spiritual harmony with each other.

What is your experience with regard to family divisions? Have you been able to make peace with them? What did we say earlier about bringing thousands around you to peace?

5. Mark 4:35-41

The Lord spoke to the wind and waves, "Peace, be still!" and there was great calm. In Jewish belief, the Lord's mastery over creation was another sign of the Messiah. Command of the sea and waves can only be issued by God. Other examples of his power over water was the parting of the Red Sea when the Israelites were fleeing the Egyptians, the parting of the Jordan when they were entering Canaan under the direction of Joshua, Jesus' walking on water, and many others such as Job 38:8-11, Ps. 65:5-6, and Ps.106. We will look these up at the end of the lesson if we have time.

The point of this passage is to show God's power over all matter of turmoil and disturbance and His ability to bring peace to every aspect of His creation.

And this is why we can trust Him to bring peace to our troubled hearts.

Read: Other Voices

The Good Shepherd Goes After the Lost Sheep

Good Shepherd, I know I wander far from Your fold at times. And when I do, I always get lost. And yet You come and seek me out every time and bring me home. Sometimes You have to use your rod to chasten me and your staff to guide me, but You always know just what I need to get me back to You. Help me to stay "home" with You and Your flock by staying close to You through worship, prayer and Scripture. And by staying close to You, let me also stay in loving companionship with the others in my life. In the name of the Father, the Son and the Holy Spirit, Amen.

VOICES FROM THE BIBLE

Read Psalm 23. Green pastures and still waters
The Lord is my shepherd.

1) Luke 15:4-7 — *We are precious even when we go astray*
2) John 10:1-16 — *The Shepherd guards the sheep*
3) John 10:25-30 — *We recognize the voice of the Shepherd*
4) Ezekiel 34:11-16 — *God will be our Shepherd*
5) John 21:15-22 — *Our Shepherd accepts what we can give*
6) Rev. 7:9-17 — *The Shepherd quenches our thirst*

OTHER VOICES

One of the most tender images of Jesus is one He supplied when referring to Himself as the Good Shepherd. This name reminds us both of our own vulnerability and Jesus' watchful, protecting care. It evokes a sense of belonging, intimacy, and trust, revealing the Good Shepherd as the One who lays down His life for His sheep. When you pray to the Good Shepherd, you are admitting your need for His care and your confidence in His ability to watch over and protect you.

Perhaps you are missing someone right now—a son, a daughter, a parent, a friend, or a spouse. Maybe that person is still alive but living in a way that estranges them from others and from God. If that is so, you can use your own sense of loss to energize your prayers, confident that Someone else is also missing them—Someone who came into this world with only one thing in mind: to seek out and save what is lost.

In ancient Israel, shepherds often slept, not in a house, but out in the open where there was good grazing for their sheep. At the end of each day, the shepherd would stand inside a low, circular sheep pen. As he called to his flock, each sheep would enter through an opening about six feet wide. Only when the last animal was safely inside the pen would the shepherd close the gate. He did this not by shutting a physical gate but by lying down in the opening with his staff and his rod beside him. During the night, the shepherd's body became the living gate through which no intruder could enter.

YOUR VOICE

1) *Why do you think Jesus describes his relationship to His people as Shepherd and sheep?*
2) *This passage from John contains both frightening and comforting images. It is frightening to think of thieves, robbers, and wolves preying on the sheep, but comforting to know that Jesus will go to any lengths to protect them. How do these images express spiritual realities?*
3) *The phrase "good shepherd" implies that there are also bad shepherds. How is it possible to tell the difference?*
4) *Describe an experience in which you recognized the voice of Jesus in your own life.*
5) *Describe ways in which Jesus has watched over and protected you as your Shepherd.*

What is causing you stress right now? What temptations are you facing? As we pray, imagine yourself in the presence of Jesus, your Good Shepherd, who stands ready with His power and might to ward off the enemy and keep you safe.

"Other Voices" from Ann Spangler, *Praying the Names of Jesus*, Zondervan, Grand Rapids, MI, 49530, 2006.

COMMENTARY & DISCUSSION

The Good Shepherd Goes after the Lost Sheep

Read Psalm 23

The Psalmist in this particular Psalm sees God as our Shepherd. How does his description of the Shepherd relate to what Christ does for us?

We are totally dependent on Him for care/restoration of our souls. He keeps us out of spiritual danger if we stay close to Him. He provides food—the Eucharist—the green pastures of the Psalm. He leads us beside still waters. Might this relate to the stillness and silence of prayer?

He leads us in the way of righteousness, which is glorifying His Kingdom and doing good works for Him on earth. The "valley of the shadow of death" in some translations reads "deep darkness." This could refer to times of depression and despair in our lives. He is with us during those times.

His rod keeps off our enemies; His staff hooks us back in line. Have you ever felt that hook? He enables us to sit at the table with our enemies and be fed. Is that happening to you here in jail?

Then the Psalmist celebrates the fact that he will dwell in the house of the Lord for the rest of his days. We should experience the same joy when we worship.

What meaning does this Psalm have to you?

1. Luke 15:4-7

One sheep cannot survive apart from the others. They literally will die. The shepherd has to leave the flock to go find him. The weak sheep is carried back to the flock on the shoulders of the shepherd as he rejoices that he has found his lost sheep.

Our Lord is this shepherd. The Scriptures record that he left the "flock," the holy, healthy souls, to go and eat with the tax collectors and sinners. When criticized by the Pharisees for eating with sinners, He told them, "Those who are well have no need of a physician, but those who are sick; I have not come to call the righteous, but sinners to repentance." (Luke 5:31-32)

Are you assured by these words and His actions that Christ (our Shepherd) is closest to you when you are lost? Have you had experience of this? Have you gotten closer to Christ during your time in prison?

2. John 10:1-16

The sheep know the shepherd's voice. Modem shepherds report that when they go into the field with a stranger and begin to call the sheep, they move toward him, but when the stranger speaks, they move away.

The thieves and robbers of our day are the money-seeking ministers who are using the gospel to promote themselves rather than minister to souls. We must be careful to distinguish between them and the true Shepherd.

Our Lord describes Himself not only as the true Shepherd but also as the Door through which we enter to find the abundant life. The way we know we have entered the Door of the Shepherd is by the life we are living. Is it an abundant one full of joy and peace, or have we been seduced by the thieves and robbers of our day who have invaded our souls with despair, depression, and addiction?

3. John 10:25-30

Christ, our Shepherd, assures us that we will never be snatched out of His hand. We may stumble and fall, but if we get up and try again and keep our eye on our Shepherd, He will not let the devil take us away from Him.

The Father gives Him the sheep because the Father is all powerful and nothing happens apart from His will. Christ identified Himself fully with the Father. He makes the point that we will not be snatched out of the Father's hand. This is the same as not being snatched out of His hand, because He and the Father are One.

The Gospel of John was written 90 years after the Resurrection. By this time, the Church had begun to understand the Trinity—that Father, Son, and Holy Spirit are one. This understanding is not in the other three Gospels.

How safe do you feel in the hands of Christ and God the Father? Can you find peace in that assurance?

4. Ezekiel 34:11-16

When the shepherds of Israel refused to feed the sheep and began to exploit and mistreat them, God assured them that He Himself will become their Shepherd.

This passage is a beautiful expression of God's concern and care: "I will seek the lost, and I will bring back the strayed, and I will bind up the crippled, and I will strengthen the weak…"

We can find these assurances of Christ's care throughout the Scriptures. We can be confident that when people (especially ministers, teachers, parents, and even friends) who we look up to fail, betray, disappoint, or let us down, the Lord takes us up and looks after us. This is referred to in Psalm 27: "For my father and my mother have forsaken me, but the Lord will take me up."

And ultimately, He is the only One we can depend on. Every other human being in our lives is at some time weak and frail and will inevitably fail us in some way. The Psalms are full of this. Human beings always betray us in big or little ways; only the Lord is steadfast and sure.

What is your experience of this? Have times of betrayal brought you closer to the Christ who is ever there to hold you up?

5. John 21:15-22

In this passage, the Lord again identifies himself as the Shepherd when He asks Peter to feed His sheep. The English language has only one word for love, so that's the word the translators used in this case. However, the Greek language has four words for love, two of which are used in this passage: *agape*, which means sacrificial love and *philia*, which means brotherly or filial love. When Jesus asks Peter if he loves Him, He uses the word *agape*. But Peter responds with the word *philia*. This is repeated two times until finally the Lord says, "Peter, do you *philia* me?" and Peter replies, "Yes, Lord I *philia* you." Then the Lord warns Peter about the way he will die, which clearly means he will be crucified, and this certainly means that Peter had finally begun to love his Lord with *agape*.

One interpretation of this passage could be that Peter was not ready to *agape* the Lord early in his discipleship. He could only *philia* Him. But after living a life dedicated to Him and being willing to be crucified, He finally was able to love Him with a sacrificial love (*agape*).

What can we learn from this passage by understanding the Greek words for love? Perhaps it means that the Lord can accept us wherever we are in our journey to Him. If we can only love Him a little, like a friend, that's ok. If we are faithful and continue to love him as best we can, we may eventually be able to love Him completely, not necessarily by being crucified as Peter was, but by living a life of sacrificial love of service and commitment.

There is another lesson we can learn from this passage. When Peter turned to John and asked Jesus what will happen to this man, Jesus said essentially: It's not your business. You come and follow me.

What does that tell us about worrying about how the Lord will deal with our brothers and sisters? God may be saying to us: their care is in My hands. You look at the Christ and follow Him.

6. Rev. 7:9-17

A final reference to Christ shepherding us is in this passage. The scene is in Heaven where a huge multitude from all nations worships before the throne of God. They are the ones who have come through the great tribulation and have been washed in the blood of the Lamb. They stand before the throne of God and serve Him night and day. And the promise is that "the one who sits on the throne will dwell among them. They shall neither hunger anymore nor thirst anymore; the sun shall not strike them nor any heat; for the Lamb who is in the midst of the throne will shepherd them and lead them to living fountains of water. And God will wipe away every tear from their eyes."

Is there any greater comfort than these words?

Read: Other Voices

God is With Me in the Detours of my Life

Lord, I don't always obey Your detour signs, so I often end up in the ditch. Help me to recognize that You are working through these detour signs to lead me to a closer walk with You. Give me the faith and love to discern the right path for my life. Give me the confidence that on the narrow road I am sometimes forced to walk, You are there with me holding my hand and leading me to You by the light of Your love. Amen

VOICES FROM THE BIBLE

Read Psalm 13. Has God forgotten me?
How long, O Lord? Wilt thou forget me forever?

1) Ex. 13:17-22 — *God leads the Israelites on a long detour*
2) Matt. 4:1-11 — *Satan tempts the Lord to bypass the detours*
3) Acts 1:1-14 — *The apostles had to take a detour*
4) Phil. 1:12-18 — *Paul's imprisonment spreads the Gospel*
5) I Cor. 13 — *Sometimes we take detours to avoid love*

OTHER VOICES

The main point that the DETOUR signpost teaches us is that God in His sovereignty may give us detours to get us on the right road. When you think about it, this is truly an encouraging thought. Because God desires even more than we do that we follow His will, He is willing and able to redirect us if we sincerely want to follow Him.

God is sovereign. Every event under the heavens is subject to His scrutiny, and nothing escapes His notice. He is not, as some have suggested, a "cosmic clockmaker" who created the universe, wound it up, and then sat back to watch it run. Because He is our "Good Shepherd," He is constantly guiding us even though we don't always recognize what He is doing.

God is in charge! Because He is all-powerful, ever-present, and all-knowing, He is able to engineer the circumstances of our lives and use them to direct us toward His will.

While the DETOUR signpost may be more prone to subjective interpretation than, say, the Scriptures, it is still one of the ways God speaks His will to us. We need to learn to hear what He says through our circumstances. Otherwise, we will become embittered slaves to the detours of life. But when we realize that God is willing and able to open or close any door to help us realize our calling and purpose in life, then the detours become friends instead of foes. There is great freedom when we begin to recognize that God opens the doors that need to be opened to get us where He wants us to be. A closed door isn't always a "no" from God, nor is an open door an automatic "yes." But we need to ask God what He is saying through our circumstances, for He does speak through open and closed doors.

YOUR VOICE

1) *In what ways has God worked through the circumstances in your life, to get you back on the right path?*
2) *Detours can be helpful in re-directing us, or they can lead us into a situation which can cause us harm. How can you discern which of these may happen when you face a "detour"?*
3) *Who do you turn to and what tools do you use to be able to properly discern which way to go?*

"Other Voices" from *Living God's Will,* Eddie Rasnake, AMG Publishers, Chattanooga, TN. 2001.

COMMENTARY & DISCUSSION

God is With Me in the Detours of My Life

Introduction

A detour sign indicates an alternate route one must follow when there is some sort of blockage on the main road. Let's look at some of the spiritual aspects of a "detour" that may come into our lives.

Jail may be a detour for you, a safe route to follow when the road ahead is too dangerous. Some of you have mentioned that coming to jail saved your life from drug addiction, an abusive marriage, or some other unmanageable situation in your life. You may have had to take other detours in your life. What is your experience in taking detours?

Read Psalm 13

The Psalmist may be experiencing a spiritual "detour." He feels the Lord has allowed him to follow the wrong road and the enemy is overpowering him. He even fears for his life as his foes close in. But he finally gets back on the right path due to his trust in God's love. He then rejoices and sings to the Lord who has dealt bountifully with him.

Have you sung to the Lord lately?

1. Ex. 13: 17-22

The longest detour in the Bible happened when God led the Israelites to the Promised Land after they left Egypt. Rather than leading them on the direct route north to Palestine, which was much shorter and quicker, He led them down around the Red Sea into the wilderness.

Why did He do this? The Scripture says that it was because the prospect of fighting the Amalekites, who they would encounter, would make them lose heart, and they would return to Egypt. But there were other reasons, too. God had many things to teach them in the wilderness. Moses would receive the Ten Commandments and the law on Mt. Sinai, they would be forced to be very dependent on God by following the cloud by day and the fire by night, and they would learn obedience by being punished for their murmuring and complaining. In fact, the generation which left Egypt did not make it to the Promised land. It was the children of the first generation, led by Joshua and Caleb, who were the ones toughened and trusting enough to cross the Jordan and enter Canaan.

Detours can be very instructive times for us. When we get off the main road, God can teach us many things. We become more dependent on Him, as did the Israelites, and learn to follow Him more closely. We may be open to seeing our own lives differently and, when we do return to the main road, have new insights about how to live.

What are some of the things you have learned on this "detour" into jail?

2. Matt. 4:1-11

The Devil was trying to persuade the Lord to take some short cuts to the Kingdom, maybe to avoid the detours it was necessary for Him to take. The Jerusalem Bible points out the temptations the devil put before our Lord in the wilderness:

1. Seeking nourishment apart from God (stones into bread)
2. Testing God for the sake of self-indulgence (casting Himself down from the temple)
3. Denying God to follow the false gods who serve the power of this world (He would be given all the kingdoms of the world if He would worship the Devil)

However, the Lord had to take several detours before completing the Father's work on earth. He had to work with stubborn disciples who didn't understand, He had to heal people to set up credibility, He had to be killed, and He had to rise again and send the Holy Spirit before the advancement of His Kingdom could begin.

Detours are necessary sometimes in order to move forward in our journey. Our Lord took these detours in order to allow His disciples to grow, learn and accept who He really was. We, too, have to get off the main road sometimes—perhaps take a detour to rest, reorganize our lives, learn some new strategies, and reassess our goals.

How is the "detour" through jail changing you?

3. Acts 1:1-14

The apostles were eager to begin the work the Lord had given them to do. But the Lord told them no; only the Father knows when you are to move ahead with the Divine commission. You must wait until the Holy Spirit descends at Pentecost. So they had to take a "detour" from their plans of bringing in the Kingdom. So what did they do while they were waiting? They had a prayer meeting, appointed an apostle to replace Judas, and did administrative work while waiting for the Pentecost feast day when they would be filled with the Holy Spirit and could continue the Lord's work.

What are you doing on this "detour" in jail? Are you reading good books, including the Bible, which can encourage and strengthen you? Are you keeping a journal of self-reflection to better understand yourself?

4. Phil. 1:12-18

Paul had to take a detour through prison. He saw that detour as having advanced the Gospel so that it had become known through the entire Roman guard. There were many guards in a Roman prison. Each of the guards probably heard the name of Christ at one time during Paul's imprisonment. It took many years for those seeds to grow, but eventually Christianity became the state religion of the Roman Empire.

Paul's detour also allowed him to write a number of the epistles while incarcerated. His imprisonment also protected him from the Jews who were plotting to kill him.

What good might come from your "detour" in prison?

5. I Corinthians 13

Sometimes we can create our own "detours' in order to avoid doing something we need to face. This passage, one of the most beautiful on love coming from the pen of Paul, could be a case in point. How many of us really want to or are able to express the type of love which he describes? "Love is patient and kind, love is not jealous or boastful; it is not arrogant or rude. Love does not insist on its own way; is not irritable or resentful; it does not rejoice at wrong but rejoices in the right. Love bears all things, believes all things, hopes all things, endures all things."?

Rather, Paul says that people can do all sorts of apparently "good" actions as "detours" to authentic love (*agape* is the Greek word he uses, which means sacrificial love). He describes some of these detours as: speaking in tongues or like angels as a way of getting attention rather than practicing love; prophesying with no thought of love; giving everything away or even being a martyr with no love in mind. Any "detour" around love has created many, if not most, of the disasters we have made for ourselves.

The only person who ever manifested the perfect characteristics of love was our Lord, and the only way we can put them into practice is by abiding in Him through a devout prayer life, Bible study, regular church attendance, and good deeds, each of which can begin to transform us into His image.

Only by Christ's love flowing through us by way of the Holy Spirit can we fulfill the command to love God above all and our neighbor as ourselves.

So, be aware of how God can use the detours in your life and cooperate with His Holy Spirit to learn and grow into His likeness. And refuse to create your own detours around the challenges you face that can make you a more Spirit filled follower of Christ.

Read: Other Voices

Dear God, Help Me to Replace my Fear with Faith in You

God, too often my fear, instead of faith in you, is what drives me and rules my life. This is a terrible and troubled world we live in, which is part of my fear, but my own circumstances of being in jail and concern over family, job, and housing also contribute to my fear. But You have promised in so many ways in Scripture that I need not be afraid because You are with me. Help me to have faith in You and believe Your Word so I can walk this journey in joyous faith, leaving fear behind. In the name of the Father, the Son and the Holy Spirit. Amen.

VOICES FROM THE BIBLE

Read Psalm 27. A song of faith
The Lord is the stronghold of my life; of whom shall I be afraid?

1) Habakkuk 3:13-19 — *When trouble appears, I trust in the Lord*
2) Isa. 41:8-14 — *Fear not, for I am with you*
3) Matt. 14:22-32 — *Peter was afraid and cried out to the Lord*
4) Phil. 2:12-16 — *Godly fear plays a role in our salvation*
5) 2 Tim.1:3-10 — *God did not give us a spirit of fear*
6) I John 4:13-18 — *Perfect love casts out fear*

OTHER VOICES

What does God value? God values character over comfort, faith over fear, mercy over judgment, justice over injustice, people over possessions, truth over falsehood, humility over pride, hope over despair, love over apathy. In other words, God values the things that will last. He has an eternal perspective. He invites us to view life from that same perspective, to believe that He is at work in history in ways that often seem mysterious to us, that He is redeeming what has been stolen and healing what has been broken.
-Kay Warren

What God Hath Promised

God hath not promised skies always blue,
Flower strewn pathways all our lives through;
God hath not promised sun without rain,
Joy without sorrow, peace without pain.

God hath not promised we shall not know
Toil and temptation, trouble and woe;
He hath not told us we shall not bear
Many a burden, many a care.

God hath not promised smooth roads and wide,
Swift, easy travel, needing no guide,
Never a mountain rocky and steep,
Never a river turgid and deep.

But God hath promised strength for the day,
Rest for the labor, light for the way,
Grace for the trails, help from above,
Unfailing sympathy, undying love.
-Annie Johnson Flint

YOUR VOICE

1) *How can your fear bring you closer to God? Should we just come to God when we are fearful?*
2) *How can I increase my faith so I can control my fears? Or do I just surrender them all to God? What helps are there for doing this?*
3) *How can I be a witness of faith/peace in such a terribly troubled world?*

COMMENTARY & DISCUSSION

Dear God, Help Me to Replace My Fear With Faith in You

Introduction

Living in today's unsettled world can bring about all types of fears, from terrorists to global warming to economic crisis and a myriad of other concerns. But what affects most of us, personally, are our fears for the dangers that can harm us and our loved ones.

What does the Scripture say about how we should deal with these fears?

Read Psalm 27:1, 14

This is a song of trust. The writer is confident of the love and protection of the Lord and admonishes us to take courage, to wait for the Lord. At times when we are most fearful, it is helpful, just to be still, to wait with your eyes on Christ. Quite often the worst fears come on us in the middle of the night, when our own personal demons begin to tempt us with guilt, panic, and remorse—the real terrors of our lives. When that occurs, we can ask Christ to send his Holy Spirit into our heart to bring us peace, trusting that He will hear our prayer.

When are you most fearful? What do you do about it?

1. Habakkuk 3:13-19

Habakkuk lived during very troubled times in Israel during the decline of one empire, Assyria, and the rise of another, the Chaldean Babylonian empire, and Israel was caught in the middle. Habakkuk had a vision of the destruction coming and knew Israel was doomed.

Habakkuk could have succumbed to terror. He could have kept asking God, "Why?" as Job did. But even though he knew devastation was coming and he didn't know why his God had allowed this, his faith did not fail. He is an inspiration to all who go through terrible times when he says the words we just read: "Yet I will rejoice in the Lord, I will joy in the God of my salvation. God the Lord is my strength. He makes my feet like hind's feet. He makes me tread upon my high places." Though expecting terror and destruction, he knew his God was greater than any earthly foe, and in this he rejoices.

What can we learn from Habbakuk?

2. Isa. 41:8-14

This was written during the Babylonian captivity, when Babylon, the great power during Isaiah's time, captured the elite of the Israelites to serve Nebuchadnezzar of Babylon. While captives in Babylon, they longed for their homeland. The beautifully poignant Psalm 137 expresses their sorrow: "By the waters of Babylon we sat down and wept, when we remembered Zion… How shall we sing the Lord's song in a foreign land?"

Isaiah, the great prophet of comfort, assures them and says the words we just read: God will not abandon them. God says in that passage three times, "Fear not." In fact the words so often used by God in the Old Testament and Christ in the New are the words, "Fear not." God further says through Isaiah, "I will strengthen you, uphold you with my victorious right hand." Again, when times are the worst is when God is nearest us.

What is your experience along these lines? Are you open to the reality that God is closest to you when you are suffering the most, the most fearful, the most threatened by some outside or inside force?

3. Matt. 14:22-32

Earlier in this chapter, Matthew had given the account of Jesus feeding 5000 men plus women and children with five loaves and two fish and taking up 12 baskets of leftover food. This apparently had a great impression on the disciples, especially Peter. So when the Lord came walking on the water to meet the disciples, Peter's faith was so strong that he said to the Lord, "If it is you (and not a ghost) bid me to come to you." The Lord said, "Come." Peter began to walk on water toward the Lord, until he looked down, saw the raging sea, and began to sink.

Why did he sink? The same reason we all sink. We turn and look at the problem and not the solution; we look at the stormy waves and not the God who created them. We look at our troubles and not at the One who can solve them.

When have you cried out to the Lord when you felt yourself sinking?

4. Phil. 2:12-16

What does it mean to work out our own salvation with fear and trembling? What does Paul mean by fear? He means the right kind of fear, because this term has to do with reverence and awe of God, who is mighty and powerful to save.

Salvation means becoming holy, wholesome, complete. We are in awe of God but also tremble with awe and gratitude when we realize He is at work in us, helping our will to work for our salvation and to transform us into His likeness.

So don't grumble or question, says Paul, but move forward in God, knowing He is working in us to make us "holy and blameless and to shine as lights in this dark world." Hold fast to the word of life, says Paul, which means holding fast to Christ.

This is the type of fear we must have: awe before the loving, merciful God who is working with us to conform us to His Image.

What are the means God gives us to enable us to do this?

5. 2. Tim. 1:3-10

The word "timidity" is closer to the word "anxiety," which is like being in a boat without a rudder or a sail with nothing to control or guide it, being tossed about here and there. Do you feel that way sometimes?

But God does not want us to be tossed about like that. Rather he has given us a spirit of power. What kind of power? It's the power of love, to truly love yourself, your neighbor, and God. This gives you power, not in the world's sense of domination, but real power in the sense of world-changing.

The only forces that have ever brought about positive change in this world are acts of love. The greatest Lover the world has ever known created more change than anyone who has ever lived. Jesus' death and resurrection changed history and put in place an institution—His Church—which has had more influence than any other force in history.

You have power when you love: you can forgive, help others, give without having to receive, and bring about true community in this world. Further, the power of love enables us to develop self-control, as Paul says, enabling us to love and care for ourselves, knowing we are loved by God.

How difficult is it for you to accept this reality and to live out the power of love that can change the world? What does God provide to enable us to do this?

6. I John 4:13-18

When we have His Spirit we have the power of love, which casts out fear. Look at all the Lord went through—rejected by His people, accused of being a criminal, given a criminal's punishment and death—but did He ever fear? Never. Because He was total love. The closer we are to Him and to His love, the less we will have of fear of failure, worry, doubt, anxiety and any other type of fear. We will have the bulwark of His love holding up our little boat in the water.

Read: Other Voices

GUIDANCE

Dear God, Give Me Strength for the Journey as I Struggle to Follow in Your Steps

Dear God, when we are weak, we know our strength comes only from You, and we know Your strength is one that can move mountains, part the Red Sea, and feed the five thousand. Help us through prayer and praise to open our hearts to receive that strength so that our lives will be empowered to overcome our addictions, to forgive those who have gotten us into trouble, and to follow in Your steps. And help us to love with the love with which You have loved us, the love which led You to the cross and enabled You to rise from the grave to bring us home to be with You, the Father, and the Holy Spirit in whose name we pray.

VOICES FROM THE BIBLE

Read Psalm 62. My soul waits in silence.
He is my rock of deliverance, my tower of strength, so I am unshaken.

1) Isaiah 40:28-31 — *They that wait upon the Lord*
2) Psalm 118:1-14 — *My strength, my song, and my salvation*
3) Eph. 3:14-19 — *He may grant you to be strengthened*
4) Col. 1:9-14 — *May you be strengthened with all power*
5) Phil. 4:11-13 — *Through him who gives me strength*

OTHER VOICES

...stillness is not merely something frightening; it is, above all, something sacred. Stillness is closely associated with the desire for "life in abundance" (John 10:10), beyond "mere survival." Most of us tend to deny the relation between death and stillness by entering a whirl of activity that makes death seem either improbable or else impossible. Stillness is like waiting respectfully and reverently. It is a renewing sense of anticipation, an overture to heavenly resurrection. In stillness, we are aware of being alive, and not dead—of having needs and temptations and of being able to face and embrace these without turning elsewhere. In stillness, we are not empty; we are not alone, we are not afraid. "In stillness (we) know that God is" (Ps. 46:11)—an experience that may occur in a split instant or develop over an entire lifetime.
-John Chrissavgis

The spiritual man is like the eagle, the other resembles the cock. The spiritual man meditates day and night on the law of the Lord, and in prayer, rises towards God; whereas the mind of the indifferent man is tied to the earth or engaged in idle thoughts. The soul of the spiritual man delights in peace, whereas the other's soul remains empty and distracted. Like the eagle, the spiritual man soars in the heights and with his soul feels God and beholds the whole world, though he be praying in the darkness of night; whereas the soul of the man who is not spiritual delights in vainglory or in riches or seeks the pleasures of the flesh.-St. Silouan the Athonite

I know not which is most profitable to me, health or sickness, wealth or poverty, nor anything else in the world. That discernment is beyond the power of men or angels, and is hidden among the secrets of our Providence, which I adore, but do not seek to fathom.
-Blaise Pascal

It is just this point of our human weakness that is meant to be the doorway to our greatest strength. Where our rope ends, God's greatest sustaining power begins. No, we cannot go through those doors of pain in our own strength… At times like these, we throw our full weight upon the living Christ and pray: "Living and loving One, I am just not up to this! It's too much for me. Take over. Take over all the way!"
-Flora Slossom Wuellner

YOUR VOICE

1) *Where does your strength come from?*
2) *Are physical and spiritual strength connected? How?*
3) *Do you practice silence or stillness in your prayer? What are the results?*
4) *Does singing lift your spirits? How often to you sing?*
5) *What is active prayer, in contrast to stillness?*

COMMENTARY & DISCUSSION

Dear God, Give Me Strength for the Journey as I Struggle to Follow in Your Steps

Introduction

Our life is a journey from cradle to grave, mostly made up of good and bad experiences. As Christians, we believe God is with us on that journey. When the going really gets rough, as it may have for you, it is a time to open up more fully to the ways in which God gives us strength for the journey to follow more closely on His path.

Read Psalm 62

God strengthens us for the journey as we practice silence.

The Psalmist waits for God in silence. We are told, by Paul, to pray at all times, which we must do, but we can't hear God unless we listen, so part of our time of prayer must be devoted to stillness and silence.

Our culture is such a noisy one that it is difficult to learn to be silent. A recent conversation with a monk at a monastery indicated that many novices leave because they simply can't stand the silence!

However, the Psalmist, in practicing silence, begins to become aware, as he says later in the Psalm, that God is his rock, salvation, fortress, deliverance and refuge. The awareness of the strength God's love gives us can come to us if we listen.

How difficult is it for you to be still and listen in this noisy, frantic world?

1. Isaiah 40:28-31

God strengthens us for the journey as we wait for Him.

Another way in which we receive strength for the journey is to "wait" on the Lord through attention to His Word, worship, and, most of all, prayer.

Waiting is another practice which our culture disdains. Women and doctors don't want to wait for babies to come on their own time schedule, so more and more Caesarean surgeries are performed to bring the babies into the world on the parents' and doctors' schedules. People are willing to pay much more money for faster internet service; they complain about waiting in lines when that is sometimes necessary. Everything from quick-fix meals to quick-fix divorces prevail in a culture which does not want to wait.

And yet Isaiah says those who wait on the Lord will gain strength. They will outdo youths who will faint and be weary, they will mount up like wings of eagles and walk and faint not.

The prophet could simply be speaking in spiritual terms, but this text could also mean that those who wait on God gain great physical strength and vigor. Many of the saints in the Christian tradition who certainly "waited" on the Lord through devout prayer and deep devotion accomplished many good deeds due to their great physical strength. St. Teresa of Avila in Spain, even in old age, was riding in wagons all over her area establishing new monasteries.

Do you realize more spiritual and/or physical strength when you wait on the Lord through prayer, worship, and Bible study?

2. Psalm 118:1-14

God gives us strength for the journey through singing.

This Psalmist affirms again and again that the steadfast love of God endures forever. He calls on the Lord, who answers him. He describes all the evil surrounding him but claims the Lord has helped him. He continues by rejoicing that the Lord is his strength and his song and has become his salvation.

God's strength that He gives to us does raise our spirits and causes us to rejoice, and singing has been an integral part of Christian worship from the beginning. Hymns, which are Christian truths set to music, inspire us, lift our spirits, and also reflect the joy that is within us.

What favorite hymn do you have that reflects God's love and strengthens you for the journey?

3. Eph. 3:14-19

God gives us strength for the journey through active prayer.

The typical way of praying for Jewish people in New Testament times was to stand with arms lifted to heaven. In contrast, to kneel indicates a deep, heartfelt concern, and Paul is conveying God's love for the Ephesians as he writes this solemn and intense prayer.

He is praying that they will be strengthened with God's Spirit in the inner man. He goes on to pray that Christ would dwell in their hearts through faith, which would give them power to comprehend and know the love of Christ, that they may be filled with all the fullness of God.

This is certainly the ultimate power and strength for us Christians. To be filled with all the fullness of God through Christ's love will prepare us for anything that may come our way on this long and perilous journey.

Pray this prayer for yourself and for all the people you love.

4. Col. 1:9-14

God gives us strength for the journey by enabling us to have patience and endurance, resulting in joy.

This letter, like most of Paul's other letters, was written from prison. Paul asks that the Colossians be strengthened with all power for endurance, patience and joy. He wants them to give thanks to the Father, who has brought them into the light of Christ.

So patience and endurance, which lead to joy, are qualities we need for the journey. How difficult is it to be patient in our spiritual life? We want to be able to achieve great heights of spiritual growth, never falling back into despair, doubt, and loss of faith. This is when endurance and patience are essential. Joy is simply the fruit of this diligence.

We need strength to persevere and not give up, in order to develop strong spiritual muscles. We must work on developing these in the calm times so that we will be ready when the difficult times come.

How are you strengthening your spiritual muscles? What tools has God given you to help you to do this? If the outcome of our struggle is joy, how can you have joy in prison?

5. Phil. 4:11-13

God gives us strength for the journey to endure all things.

This letter was written to the church at Philippi in Macedonia. It was the first church established in Europe. Paul was very close to the Philippians, and the very first hymn in Christian tradition is recorded in this letter. (Phil. 2:5-11)

Paul was in prison when he wrote the letter, awaiting trial and knowing his death would come soon. However, some of his most beautiful and courageous statements are recorded in this epistle.

He says he is not complaining of anything; he has learned to be content in any condition. He knows how to be put down and built up. He knows the sense of having plenty, having nothing, being hungry and being full.

He claims he can accept and endure any sort of condition through Christ who gives him strength.

How many of us can come near to saying what Paul is saying? We live in a country in which the general attitude is that each of us is entitled to all we can get and should not suffer any hardship or deprivation of any type for any reason. How many of us are content through and in Christ, in any situation in which we find ourselves?

You are in prison, as Paul was when he wrote most of his epistles. How do you feel about being deprived of all you had when you were out in the world? Will you feel differently after you are released and return to your former situation?

Read: Other Voices

Dear God, Help Me to Forgive in order to Repair Damaged Relationships

Dear God, I know forgiving others is essential for my own spiritual growth. Only by forgiving others can I be forgiven by You. And yet when I have been harshly treated by someone I have trusted, I find it difficult to forgive and begin to trust again. Guide me on the path to reconciliation so that I may be at peace with others and be forgiven by You for the many ways I have rejected Your love and guidance. In the name of the Father, the Son and the Holy Spirit. Amen.

VOICES FROM THE BIBLE

Read Psalm 51. Have mercy on me, O Lord.
Create in me a clean heart, O God.

1) Deut. 21:18-21 — *A disobedient son is stoned*
2) Psalm 55 — *Bitterness and rage; not forgiveness and love*
3) Matt 18:21-35 — *Don't give up on forgiving*
4) Luke 15:11-32 — *A wayward son and a forgiving father*
5) Luke 23:32-34 — *For they know not what they do*

OTHER VOICES

Forgiving to the point of being grateful for the possible growth from the hurt is not a magical fix painlessly bringing psychological and spiritual health. A modern saint, Martin Luther King, Jr., didn't find that the police dogs bit less or the jail doors suddenly opened when he could forgive the Birmingham police. Forgiveness to the point of gratitude for growth is not a way to manipulate God and have things our way but to bring healing in His time and His way. God doesn't promise to eliminate our problems but He does promise to help us face them and grow from them until we can pray the serenity prayer: "God grant me the serenity to accept the things I cannot change, the courage to change the things I can, and the wisdom to know the difference."
-Matthew Linn

We must develop and maintain the capacity to forgive. He who is devoid of the power to forgive is devoid of the power to love. There is some good in the worst of us and some evil in the best of us. When we discover this, we are less prone to hate our enemies.
-Martin Luther King, Jr.

Forgiveness is not always easy. At times, it feels more painful than the wound we suffered to forgive the one who inflicted it. And yet, there is no peace without forgiveness.
-Marianne Williamson

Forgiveness isn't just a blessing you deliver to another human being. Forgiveness is also a gift you give yourself.
-Robin S. Sharma

For me, forgiveness and compassion are always linked: how do we hold people accountable for wrongdoing and yet at the same time remain in touch with their humanity enough to believe in their capacity to be transformed?
-bell hooks

YOUR VOICE

1) *Is it necessary to forgive yourself before you can forgive others? Why or why not?*
2) *Is it difficult to accept God's forgiveness of you?*
3) *What do self-respect and affirmation of yourself have to do with forgiveness of someone who wronged you?*
4) *When and why is forgiveness a process and not a one-time event?*

COMMENTARY & DISCUSSION

Dear God, Help Me to Forgive in order to Repair Damaged Relationships

Introduction

Forgiveness is the first and major step to spiritual growth. Forgiveness is at the heart of the Lord's Prayer, and we cannot get close to God if we are not in the process of forgiving the one who has wronged us. A lack of forgiveness can even cause physical illness if the bottled-up anger and resentment are not resolved.

However, forgiveness can be a lifelong process. It is not a one-time event if our wounds are significant. And sometimes the most difficult task of all is to forgive ourselves.

We will look at Scripture to go more deeply into the forgiveness process.

Read Psalm 51

This is David's prayer of repentance after having Bathsheba's husband killed and committing adultery with her. The Holy Spirit leaves our heart when we sin, and David requested three times for the Lord to restore it, as we read in verses 10, 11 and 12. This is why David is called "a man after God's own heart." Even though he committed terrible sins, he then devoutly and sincerely repented of what he had done.

When we do something wrong and need God's forgiveness, we also have to ask that God restore the Holy Spirit in our hearts. This will restore our relationship with God that has been broken.

How difficult is it for you to admit that you have done something wrong? Sometimes we can be in denial about it.

1. Deut. 21:18-21

This was a very drastic way to treat wrongdoing, especially to a son. In Old Testament times, under the Old Covenant, great emphasis was put on piety of children toward their parents. This type of punishment was justified. This is in extreme contrast to Jesus' parable of the Prodigal Son, which we will discuss in this lesson. This will show the stark difference between the Law of the Old Covenant and the grace and love of the New Covenant.

What do you think of corporal punishment of your children? Is it ever justified?

2. Psalm 55

This man is obsessed with his enemies and has been betrayed by a friend. There is no hint of forgiveness on his part. In fact, he sees no need to take on the task of reconciliation himself. Instead, he is asking God to "destroy their plans, confuse their tongues." And when he begins to moan the loss of his companion, his friend with whom he once walked in the temple, he asks God to let the friend die and go to Sheol!

Have you ever been that angry with someone?

Then the Psalmist affirms that the Lord will save him and will deliver his soul.

He ends the Psalm by saying, "cast your burden on the Lord and he will save you, he will never permit the righteous to be moved."

If the Psalmist considers himself to be righteous (that is the implication) how could be not see that he must make an offer toward reconciliation?

When we have been wronged, as Christians, do we call on God to punish the one who has wronged us? It is tempting!

3. Matt. 18:21-35

Let's look at what Jesus said about forgiveness. Seven was considered a perfect number in Biblical times. So for Jesus to say to forgive seventy times seven—an infinite number—He meant you should never stop forgiving. Then He tells this parable. The king represents God, the Heavenly Father who forgives us as the king forgave the servant.

How difficult is it for you to forgive? If you have had some major childhood trauma or even trauma in adult life, there are certain steps you must take to begin the process of forgiveness.

Your first reaction may be anger as you have been wronged, wounded, or treated like an object or as someone who has little value. So don't try to forgive until you can do some repairing of yourself. This involves opening yourself up to God's love. You are precious in his sight—God doesn't make junk. There is a Jewish rabbi saying that goes, "Every time a human being walks down the street, a thousand angels go before him shouting: 'Make way for the image of God'." You are of ultimate importance to Him, and He is eager to nourish, love and heal you.

Do extensive prayer for healing and any other action you need to feel better about yourself, such as talking with good friends and/or with a minister.

As you heal, you can begin the second task of forgiving by trying to see the offender in a compassionate way—trying to imagine what they might be going through and why they needed to hurt you. As you grow in self-acceptance, recovering your own healthy self, you can begin to have compassion and empathy toward the one who abused you or offended you.

This can be a long and involved process and may last a lifetime if you have been severely wounded or abused. God does not demand a quick fix in this regard. He doesn't say you have to forgive this person completely by next Wednesday. As long as you are in the PROCESS, He honors your intention.

Then realize that the struggle to heal and forgive can make you stronger. Willa Cather said, "Some things you learn in calm, some in storm." Affliction from any source can either bless you or cripple you, depending on how you respond. Suffering with Christ in your heart and surrendering to His healing love can be paradise; suffering alone can be hell.

What sort of progress are you making in the process of forgiving one who has wounded you?

4. Luke 15:11-32

When the son asked for his share of the forgiveness, he was essentially insulting his father, implying that he wanted what his father would leave him after the father's death. Yet the father willingly gave it to him.

The son took the money and fled to today's equivalent of Las Vegas, lived the wild life, used up the money, and went hungry. The only job he could find was slopping pigs. This was a major offense to the Jewish audience, who were not allowed to eat pork and who believed that anyone who even owned pigs was of the devil.

Reduced to slopping pigs, the young son came to himself. In his desperation, he would gladly have eaten what the pigs were eating. He said to himself, "How many of my father's hired servants have bread enough and to spare, but I perish here with hunger?" He then repented (the Greek word for repentance, *metanoia,* means to turn around) and returned to his father's house to offer himself as a servant, acknowledging that he had sinned against heaven and earth.

But the Father sees him coming, and what does he do? He runs to meet hm. This was not done in Jewish families at that time. The young man who left home would have been an outcast and possibly subject to the punishment mentioned in Deuteronomy. But his father lovingly embraces him, gives him a robe, a symbol of honor; a ring, a sign of authority; and sandals, which servants never wore. He restored him to his full status as a son.

In celebration, they killed the fatted calf for a homecoming feast. What other Lamb has been sacrificed in the Gospel to bring us back to the Father?

The father welcomes him with rejoicing beyond the youngest son's wildest dreams and offers him forgiveness beyond his expectations.

This is the most perfect parable of God's love that Jesus told, and this is how our Heavenly Father forgives us when we are willing to turn and come home.

What does this mean to you?

5. Luke 23:32-34

These are the most powerful words of forgiveness that the world has ever known. Jesus is forgiving those who judged, condemned and crucified him, and by extension forgiving each of us, because so often in our lives we have contributed to Christ's suffering due to our sins. Along with the Jewish leaders at that time, quite often we do not realize the toll it takes on our souls and the affront it is to God.

This is the reason the Church was established as sort of a cocoon to contain, strengthen, guide us into the way of Christ, bring us into awareness and watchfulness, and keep us ever mindful of the ways that we can separate ourselves from God.

So all healing begins in the heart of the Lord's prayer—asking for the forgiveness God so freely gives to enable us to know we are loved beyond all imagining so that we can turn, forgive, and be at peace with our brothers and sisters.

Read: Other Voices

Open to Me Your Healing Love as You Did to Women in the New Testament

God, we know You understand our vulnerability as women, how often we are victimized, seen as second-class citizens, and discriminated against. We also know that some of Your most faithful followers while You were on earth were women. We, as women, are especially open to Your healing touch and your call to become all that You want us to become in You. Come into our hearts and our lives and heal us, draw us closer to You and guide us in living a life that will reflect Your love to this broken and bleeding world. In the name of the Father, the Son and the Holy Spirit, we pray.

VOICES FROM THE BIBLE

Read Psalm 131. Like a child in its mother's arms, I rest in the arms of God.
I have calmed and quieted my soul, like a weaned child with its mother.

1) John 2:1-11   *Do whatever He tells you to do*
2) Luke 10:38-42   *She has chosen the better part*
3) John 11:17-36   *I believe You are the Messiah.*
4) Luke 13:11-17   *Woman, you are set free.*
5) John 8:2-11   *Neither do I condemn you*
6) John 20:11-18   *Go to my brothers and tell them*

OTHER VOICES

The following quotes are from *Sister Images*, Mary Zimmer, Abingdon Press, Nashville, 1993.

Martha's absolute task orientation is what Jesus rebukes. She is literally busy with too many things. Especially for women who are overwhelmed, what Mary does is choose the better part—the time for a personal relationship with Christ, which develops in time spent apart in study and communion. It is this kind of time that nourishes us and allows us to learn from the deepest part of ourselves what limits to put on the "many things" that the world brings to us.

The bent-over woman was healed because she was faithful. She had been coming, perhaps with fainter and fainter hope, all those eighteen years. For her, and for us, sometimes the most significant healing comes when we least expect it and from people who surprise us with their compassion. The power of God's healing, the lifting of our burdens, stands ready. We have to be ready for the changes that such healing brings. The story of the bent-over woman promises that there is healing available beyond religious practice and our own expectations.

Brennan Manning has said that as humans we often bargain with God by saying, "Lord, if I change, you'll love me, won't you?" The Lord's reply is always, "You don't have to change so I'll love you; I love you so you'll change." This is the message of Jesus to the woman accused of adultery and to all of us. Whether we are the ones being accused or the ones standing with stones, the wisdom of Jesus can transform our way of thinking about sexuality, and we can become responsible for ourselves and our behavior.

There is some significance in what convinced Mary Magdalene that Jesus stood before her. She does not recognize Him by appearance. She does not recognize His voice in His question. What she recognizes is His voice calling her name. When her name is called by the risen Christ, she knows the new truth of the resurrection. Jesus then makes Mary Magdalene the first evangelist in the resurrection. He sends her out to tell the disciples that He would ascend to God. She does so immediately. Her witness is simple, but profound, in light of the Crucifixion: "I have seen the Lord."

YOUR VOICE

1) *In what ways can I choose "the better part" in my daily life?*
2) *How can I arrange my daily schedule so that I can include that most important activity of all, which is being with God? (through prayer, Bible study, worship, etc.)*
3) *In what ways am I "bent over" and need healing from the Lord?*
4) *Too often I doubt God's love for me. How can I increase my awareness of it and develop a deeper trust in His infinite and all-compassionate care for me?*
5) *In what ways can I be an apostle—one sent from the Lord?*

COMMENTARY & DISCUSSION

God, Please Open to Me Your Healing Love as You Did to Women in the New Testament

Introduction

Women in the Bible play a critical role. A woman, Eve, brought evil into the world, and a woman, Mary, brought God into the world. Women were also very close companions of Jesus. They fed him, housed him, and were some of His most loyal followers. His favorite place to stay was at Martha and Mary's, whose brother He raised from the dead. Women were the last at the cross when Jesus was crucified (except for John), and the first ones at the tomb to anoint His body.

Women have special spiritual gifts. They can be very open to God, intuitive and receptive. Women without God can become very evil, conniving, and emotionally destructive because of their great spiritual potential; e.g. Jezebel, Herod's wife, etc. But also, some of the greatest of the saints were women: St. Teresa, St. Therese of Avila, etc.

Let's see what we can learn from the New Testament about their relationship and response to our Lord and thus how we can receive His healing touch.

Read Psalm 131

This is the only Psalm which mentions a mother, which is why I had you read it. This is such a beautiful image of a young child who no longer needs the mother's breast but can lay content in her arms. This is an image of how we should be with God at times, no longer demanding answers to our prayers but simply being content to dwell in the shadow of His wings and be at peace.

Is this a helpful Psalm to read while you are "resting" here in jail?

1. John 2:1-11

This is the first of seven signs Jesus did in His ministry to prove His Messiahship. The other six are: curing the nobleman's son, healing the paralytic, feeding the 5000, walking on water, opening the eyes of the blind, and raising Lazarus.

A woman, His mother, participated in this miracle and actually provoked it.

A wedding feast always had plenty of wine. When the host ran out of wine, it was a disaster for him. A woman, sensitive to the situation, tells her Son: "They have no wine." Jesus answers, "What is that to me?" He says his time (to show himself as Christ) has not come. But there was a need, and Mary was asking on behalf of those in need.

There were six water jars available that were normally used for purification rites of the Jews. The number seven is a perfect number in the Scriptures. The six jars indicate an imperfect or incomplete number. This represented the incomplete or imperfect Jewish law, which was completed by the coming of Christ who would fulfill the law and bring salvation to the world.

Further, water could represent the Old Covenant or Old Testament law being transformed into wine, the New Covenant of salvation. The overabundance of wine in this situation could show the overabundance of God's grace.

So, a woman prompted her Son to meet the needs of the people at the wedding. She tells the servants, "Do what He tells you to do." She could be saying that to us: "Do what my Son tells you to do." How can we hear and obey?

2. Luke 10:38-42

Jesus was visiting His favorite family in Bethany. Martha was busy preparing Him a wonderful meal while Mary was sitting at His feet, listening. He says to Martha when she fusses that she needs help: "Only one thing is needful. Mary has chosen the better part."

He could have meant: You only need one dish. Why are you fixing so many? Or he could have meant: the only thing really needed is what Mary is doing, sitting at My feet listening to Me.

What do you think He meant?

Is He putting down serving? Being too busy? Do we need to choose which to emphasize in our lives? Yes, because prayer—sitting at Jesus' feet—should always come first in our day, in order to get our priorities right and discern what the Lord's will is for us that day.

Do we need to both sit at Jesus feet and prepare food for our family? Yes, we must both pray and attend to the needs of our family, but we need FIRST to sit at the Lord's feet in order to be properly guided through the rest of the day.

3. John 11:17-36

This is part of the account of Our Lord raising Lazarus from the grave, but we want to focus on the roles of Mary and Martha, which are reversed in this passage compared to the passage from Luke. The encounter with Martha, the one so busy cooking, occurs when Jesus is on His way to raise her brother. In this passage, she is focused on the wisdom and power of Jesus; cooking is the last thing on her mind.

She shows tremendous faith and confidence in Him, saying, "I know whatever you ask of God, God will give you." He tells her, "I am the resurrection and the life. He who believes in me, though he may die, shall live." She confesses that He is the Christ and that He is fully able to heal her brother.

Mary, on the other hand, is falling apart. She stays at home weeping and does not run out to meet her Lord. He has to come to her, and in His compassion He weeps with her.

There are two responses here: Martha runs to meet Him and says, "I know you can do anything." Mary, weeping, stays behind, and when He comes near to the house and encounters her, she is critical of Him, saying: "Lord, if you had been here, my brother would not have died."

What would you have done in these circumstances?

There are two ways to react to bad events or circumstances: one is to run to God, affirming your faith in Him and trusting that He can bring good out of the situation. Another is to weep, complain, and blame God for what is happening.

Jesus, however, in His compassion, is with us however we respond. If we turn to Him and trust Him to bring good out of the evil in our lives, He assures us that He is on our side because He is the Resurrection and the Life. If we can only weep, moan, and complain, He will come to us as He did Mary, and in His compassion will weep with us.

4. Luke 13:11-17

The bent over woman did not ask to be healed. Maybe she had given up, as she had been bent over for 18 years. Healing on the Sabbath was forbidden by the Jews. They saw it as work, and you did not work on the Sabbath. But Jesus in His mercy saw this woman's suffering and broke the Sabbath rule to heal her. Healing on the Sabbath was one of the reasons He was crucified. The other is that He called Himself God.

Has God or something good from God ever come to you when you aren't expecting it?

5. John 8:2-11

Again, Jesus breaks the law to minister to a woman. The Scribes and Pharisees wanted to trap Him. Either He would be forced to break the law by forgiving her, or He would be accused of having no mercy on sinners if He allowed the stoning. They wanted to have something with which to accuse Him. So Jesus said nothing—he simply wrote in the sand. What do you think He wrote?

No one knows. Some theories: He wrote out the ten commandments, which all the accusers had violated at least once, or he wrote the names of the accusers who themselves had committed adultery. After writing in the sand, He said, "The one who is without sin among you, cast the first stone." They began leaving, the oldest (wisest, or most guilty?) first. After the accusers left, Jesus said to the woman, "Where are your accusers? Has anyone condemned you?" "No one, sir," she answered. "Neither do I. Go and sin no more."

God forgives us when we sin but warns us not to take advantage of His mercy and keep sinning. How should we behave after God forgives us? What do we do to be stronger next time and resist temptation?

6. John 20:11-18

Mary Magdalene was very close to the Lord. Tradition says He delivered her from seven devils. She was the first at the tomb and the first one to whom He showed Himself in His resurrected body. He had a different body, which we will also have when we are resurrected. "Do not touch me!" He said to Mary, for they had a different relationship than they had in the past. He was preparing to ascend to God, and He would no longer be the earthly teacher but rather the divine Son of God who at Pentecost would send the Holy Spirit to all his disciples. He then instructed her to "Go tell my brothers" that He would ascend to "my Father and your Father and my God and your God."

Thus, a woman becomes the first to announce the good news of the Resurrection. The Church calls her the "apostle to the apostles." A woman is the first to receive and pass on the good news of the Resurrection because of her bravery to be the first at the tomb.

Read: Other Voices

Dear God, Help Me to Realize that You and I are Co-creators of My Life

Dear Lord, help me realize that I am a co-creator with You of my life. You have given me a free will, and unless I choose to grow and be like You, You honor my choice and do not force me. But help me to have courage to open up to You and manifest a deep and profound faith in You, which will allow You into my life to bring about all the miracles You want to accomplish in me. In your Son's name, who worked countless miracles on earth for those who truly had faith. Amen

VOICES FROM THE BIBLE

Read Heb. 11:1-7. A lesson on faith
Now faith is the assurance of things hoped for, the conviction of things not seen.

1) John 6:15-21 — *Walking on rough seas*
2) Matt. 15:21-28 — *A gentile woman seeks healing*
3) Matt 8:5-13 — *Not even in Israel have I found such faith!*
4) Luke 17:11-19 — *A Samaritan gives thanks*
5) Luke 18:35-42 — *A blind man demonstrates his faith*
6) John 15:1-7 — *Abide in me and ask what you will.*

OTHER VOICES

The faith that Jesus asks for from the outset of his public life... and throughout His subsequent career is that act of true, self-abandonment by which people no longer rely on their own strength and policies but commit themselves to the power and guiding word of Him in whom they believe. Jesus asks for this faith especially when He works his miracles...When faith is strong it works wonders and its appeal is never refused, especially when it asks for forgiveness of sins and for that salvation of which it is the necessary condition.
-The Jerusalem Bible

The effective prayer or the "energized personal request" (Greek-*energeo desis*) of a righteous man is very strong and capable of producing righteous results. One who is walking with God, having been made righteous by faith in Christ and daily walking in that right relationship, is energized by God to pray the will of God. As a result, he or she sees God answer prayer, like Elijah in the days of Ahab. Elijah was a man like any of us, with fears and failures, weaknesses and weariness, but he had a right heart toward God. He surrendered himself to do the will of God and listened carefully to the word of God so that God could use him to accomplish His purposes in Israel. He can use us to do the same today and see His purposes accomplished in our personal lives, in our families, in our churches, and in our communities.
-Rick Shepherd

YOUR VOICE

1) *How can I increase my faith in God?*
2) *How do I know what to pray for?*
3) *How can I truly abide in Christ?*
4) *In what ways can I be a co-creator with God to make changes in my life?*

COMMENTARY & DISCUSSION

Dear God, Help Me to Realize that You and I are Co-creators of My Life

Introduction

Mother Teresa, the saintly nun who nursed the poor and dying in Calcutta, once said that we shouldn't always and exclusively pray that God will change the circumstances of our lives; rather we should pray that God will change us so that we can make the changes we want to happen, consistent with His will.

However, when we do pray to Him, we should keep two things in mind. First, He is the God of the impossible and can bring about miracles in response to our prayers. Second, He will not do this unless we manifest the faith in Him to do so and ask that His will be done.

Let's look at Scriptures with relation to faith, miracles and God's power:

Read Heb. 11:1-7, 32-40

Faith has to do with the whole person. It is not an intellectual assent to a certain theological statement. The letter to the Hebrews, particularly this chapter, was written to Jewish Christians who were under severe persecution. That's why the writer says that faith is "the assurance of things hoped for and the conviction of things not seen."

He was giving them the assurance that God was in charge and protecting their future even though it seemed so frightening. The writer then gives examples of Old Testament persons who manifested profound faith—women even received their dead by resurrection! What powerful faith!

Emily Dickenson, the 19th century reclusive poet, once wrote, "You cannot hold back a dawn." Our faith in God and in His power must have that same lack of doubt. Do you believe that the sun will rise tomorrow? Then with that same faith, believe in God's power to bring about miracles in His time, in His way, according to His will, and prompted by our faith!

These Scriptures prove the power of our faith and God's might:

1. John 6:15-21

This passage is evidence of Jesus' power over creation. He can alter all its laws for His purposes. He does these miracles to prove to His disciples that He is truly the Messiah.

However, when they first saw Him coming across the water, they were frightened. They had not yet gained the faith to trust Him in all circumstances. He had to assure them, "It is I, do not be afraid." This phrase is spoken by God and Christ more often than any other phrase in the Bible.

Perhaps you have experienced an occasion when God is approaching you or working in your life and you did not recognize Him.

Or how often have you heard the words with which He comforted His disciples when you were in a frightening situation or experienced something which made you feel out of control?

2. Matthew 15:21-28

Tyre and Sidon were up on the coast near gentile country. Jesus goes there with His disciples, possibly for a retreat. A gentile woman hears He is near and comes to ask healing for her daughter who was possessed by a demon. The Jews viewed gentiles as dogs. The Greek in this text indicates that the disciples say, "Let her go with her request granted." But Jesus begins a dialogue with her and tells her that He is sent only to the Jews, the lost house of Israel, and it is not fair to give the children's bread to the little dogs (the term Jews used to refer to the Samaritans). She continues to plead for Him to heal her sick daughter and says, "Even the dogs eat the crumbs from their master's table." And the Lord answers her, "O woman, great is your faith! Be it done for you as you desire."

She confronted the great teacher and even argued with Him. She had full faith that He could heal her daughter. And He complements her on her great faith as instrumental in her daughter's healing.

She surmounted two barriers to being heard by this famous rabbi: she was a woman and a gentile.

What are some of the barriers you have that can block your healing?

3. Matthew 8:5-13

The Centurion, a Roman officer who heard of this miracle worker, came to plead for Him to heal his servant. Jesus offered to come to his house, but the Centurion showed such humility and faith that he simply asked the Lord to say the word and his servant would be healed. Jesus did so and then marveled that He had not seen such faith, even in Israel.

Why is humility necessary for healing?

4. Luke 17:11-19

Jesus was traveling in an area near Samaria. Ten lepers happened to see him and apparently were aware of His reputation. They called to Him to have pity on them. He heard them and ordered them to go and show themselves to the priests. Why would he have them do that? Mosaic Law says this is required to be fully healed and to allow them back into the community.

As they went on their way, they were cleansed. The only one to return to thank him was a Samaritan who threw himself at Jesus' feet in gratitude. Jesus asks why, out of the ten who were healed, did only this foreigner return to give thanks? He then told the Samaritan to stand up and go on his way, "Your faith has saved you."

Is there a relationship between spiritual and physical healing? Else why did our Lord think it necessary for the lepers to go to the priest?

5. Luke 18:35-42

The blind man is very insistent that Jesus heal him. He ignores the scolding of the crowd who tell him to keep quiet and continues to cry out, "Son of David, have pity on me." Jesus stops and has the man brought to Him and asks what He can do for him. The blind man says, "Let me see again." Jesus says, "Receive your sight. Your faith has saved you." Such a poignant, touching scene!

Why is spiritual blindness so much worse than physical blindness? Our Lord often healed the physically blind but was not able to heal the spiritual blindness of the religious leaders of his day.

We have discussed Jesus' healing of a variety of people, all outside the normal group of that culture: a Centurion's servant, a gentile woman, a Samaritan leper, and a blind man.

Why do you think the Gospel writers might have included all of these?

To show the universality of our Lord's compassion. To show also the humility and faith of those outside the fold of the Jewish religion, contrasting them at times to the lack of faith of those within the fold.

Do we see that contrast today between church members and those outside the church?

6. John 15:1-7

Our Lord uses the image of a vine in this passage. All His disciples were familiar with this image, as grapevines were an essential crop in their day. They knew that for the vine to produce its maximum crop, it had to be pruned; i.e. cut back to get rid of the vines that were not productive. The Lord then applied this image to their (and our) lives. We have to be made single-minded and devoted to the Christ, abiding in Him, in order to "produce fruit," i.e., bring others to Him. Sometimes the pruning may take the form of hardships, such as coming to jail, losing friends, lack of money, and/or surrendering our old lifestyle. The Lord can use all of these to "prune" us, to draw us closer to Him, and to enable us to be a more productive and effective witness for His kingdom.

If we do not unite ourselves to Him, we spiritually wither and die. What are the means He has given us to abide in Him?

A deep and regular prayer life is the most essential, along with Bible study to support this prayer life (the Bible tells us who God is and to Whom we are praying), regular church attendance both here when it is offered and when you leave, and connecting with spiritual friends who nurture and feed you. Avoid the troublemakers and naysayers.

Finally, believe deep down in your heart that God will bring about the miracles you pray for, according to His will, in His time, and when you are ready.

Be careful what you pray for. Someone once said that we will spend all of eternity thanking God for the prayers He didn't answer!!

Read: Other Voices

God, Help Me to Trust You in Times of Doubt

Gracious God, help me to know You are for me, not against me. That You are beside me and offer me unlimited strength and courage. Help me to trust that You will provide me insight and inspiration to confront and solve the problems I face. Help me to believe that You will give me peace when my heart is distressed by the turbulence of our times, that You will comfort me when I am afraid, and that you will make me a conqueror when I feel overwhelmed. I thank You for the power of faith coming into my mind and heart. I trust in You, dear God, for You are my Lord and Saviour. Amen.

VOICES FROM THE BIBLE

Read Psalm 37:1-11. God never fails us.
Commit your fate to God, trust in him and he will act.

1) Ex. 14:1-31   *Moses learns to trust*
2) Luke 1:26-38   *Mary trusts the words of the angel*
3) Matt. 6:25-34   *A condition for trust*
4) Matt 14:22-33   *Peter's trust turns to doubt*
5) Rom. 8:31-38   *Beyond trust to "more than conquerors"*

OTHER VOICES

Trust is handing over our greatest possession—our heart—and asking someone to honor and protect it. It's an intimate, frightening offering, especially in a world where experience has taught us that trust is a risk. We've had our trust tampered with, dropped, walked on, misused, and broken into pieces. Handing it over again goes against our self-protective nature… Jesus is compassionate with our concern. He has seen our heart being carelessly mishandled in the past, and He has mourned with us over the injustice. It is why He asks us to put our faith and trust in Him, the one who will not disappoint (Romans 5:5) or ever have plans for us that are anything but right and good (Jeremiah 29:11). He knows that, because of how our heart has been hurt in the past, we may not feel safe putting our trust in Him. But our desire to trust Him communicated through this simple prayer, I want to trust You, shows our heart's intent. And He will meet us right where we are.
-Lisa Whittle

God does not ask for resignation based on acquiescence in the absence of a better option. Nor does God ask for reluctant, grudging submission. What God wants is surrender based on love and trust. This is what we see in the life of Jesus. And it is what we see in the life of His mother, Mary—the woman the Bible describes as "most highly favored" because she dared to trust the promise that God was with her and for her.
-David G. Benner

Sometimes a wounded person finds the necessary help within a sharing group he or she trusts. When Jesus prepared to heal someone, he often gathered around him two or three trusted friends. They were not giants of faith but ordinary human beings who were present as a consenting community. They were not the source of healing, but I believe their presence helped increase the focused power of the healing. This enhanced, focused power of healing is still available when two, three, or more Christians gather in the presence of the living Jesus Christ.
-Flora Slosson Wuellner

YOUR VOICE

1) *Do you find it difficult to trust God? To trust anyone?*
2) *What are some of the steps you can take to learn to trust?*
3) *What in your life has weakened your ability to trust? Describe these experiences in your journal.*
4) *What does forgiveness of others have to do with restoring trust?*

COMMENTARY & DISCUSSION

God, Help Me to Trust You in Times of Doubt

Introduction

When we go through hard times, we can take one of two attitudes toward God: we either blame Him for our troubles and turn our back on Him or we humble ourselves, take responsibility for what we are suffering (to the extent it is our fault) and grow in trust and love toward Him.

However, one of the obstacles to trust is that we are not sure where God will lead us. Maybe He will lead us to some new path of service that we are not sure we are ready for: maybe to repair a relationship that is really troubling us or to turn away from the false supports that we have chosen to keep us going.

To trust or not to trust in God's divine love is a fundamental decision we all have to make. At the same time, we must recognize that dependence on and trust in God is not a sign of weakness but of lasting strength.

Here are some people who doubted and/or trusted God.

Read Psalm 37:1-11

Look at some of the key words and phrases in this Psalm: wait, trust, delight, be still, be meek, and don't be angry and fret. "Trust" may be the key word in this Psalm, because to lean on, look to, and trust in the Lord will enable us to wait, be still, be meek, and not be angry and fret.

Don't let the bad judges eat up your soul or bad so-called friends get you down. Give the worry and the resentment to God.

Trust in the Lord, delight in Him. How are these related?

What does "be still" mean? Quiet yourself, your mind, your soul, and listen. Do the prayer of quiet. By listening to God in silence, you become more aware of His love, which enables you to grow in love and trust.

Never doubt that the Lord can bring forth good in your life.

1. Ex. 14:1-31

Moses was the great deliverer of the Israelites. This passage describes his assurance that the Lord will fight for them and deliver them from the Egyptians. He urged them to be calm and still. This seemed an impossible attitude to the Israelites as the Egyptian horses were pounding after them before a sea they could not cross. But Moses was not daunted, and with his full trust in God, he stretched out his hand over the sea; it was drawn back and the Israelites walked through on dry ground.

But the great deliverer did not always have such a powerful faith and trust in God. When God first called him, he had doubts and needed to be convinced that he could do what God commanded him to do. Read Ex. 4:1-20. Even Moses had to learn to trust God before he could appear before Pharaoh and call down the plagues to force Pharaoh to let His people go.

After Moses had grown in tremendous faith and trust in God, he not only delivered the Israelites from the Egyptians, he led them through the wilderness and received the Ten Commandments on Mt. Sinai. However, his faith and trust wavered at one point, and God punished him by not allowing him to lead his people into the Promised Land. God did not let Moses accomplish this final task because Moses had lacked the faith and trust to follow God's command to bring forth water from the rock at Meribah. Instead, he struck it twice with his rod, disobeying God in anger and bringing glory to himself.

Joshua led the next generation of Israelites into the Promised Land. They had learned to trust God in the wilderness with the care and guidance He gave their fathers. As evidence of this trust, when they approached the Jordan river to cross into the Promised land, they trusted God so much that the priests stepped into the river even before the waters parted. They believed what God had promised and were acting on that promise. (See Joshua 4:14-16.)

What practices do we do in order to deepen our faith and trust in God? We must experience His love and care by staying close to Him through daily devotions, spiritual readings, prayer, Church attendance and obedience to Him. Only by growing in awareness of God's love can we trust Him on the uncertain path before us to give us courage to take that first step into a new life, a new job, a rehab center.

2. Luke 1:26-38

Mary was asked by the angel to do the impossible; have a baby without intercourse with a man. She asked a question, "How can this be when I have no husband?" Gabriel explained that the Holy Spirit would come upon her and overshadow her. He also told her that her cousin Elizabeth who had been barren was also having a child, for with God nothing is impossible. Mary had no further questions and said, "Let it be to me exactly as God wants." What faith! What trust!

Why would such a young, unmarried girl agree to such an astonishing request? If we look at the early tradition that gives us some information about Mary, perhaps we can understand her immediate willingness to do the "impossible." These stories were later discounted, but they remain part of an older Church tradition that some churches still honor.

These older sources claim that Mary was born of very holy parents, but her mother had long been barren before conceiving Mary. Because of their gratitude to God for giving them a child, little Mary was presented to the Temple at the age of three and remained there until she became of age to marry. At that time, she was betrothed to Joseph, an older person who was called to care for her.

This tradition might indicate that because she remained in the Temple, learning about God and growing closer to Him for so many years, she became very holy and devoted to God. This enabled her to have the faith and trust necessary to take on the task God asked of her.

What do we learn from this? Again, we need to be very close to God, nurturing our relationship with Him and our love for Him and being open to His love for us that enables us to trust Him.

Can you trust someone who shows no love for you?

3. Matt. 6:25-34

Jesus is warning us about being overanxious about earthly things. Certainly, we have to be thoughtful about providing for ourselves, but we should not be anxious. There is so much emphasis in our culture on food, clothing, and material goods that we begin to confuse our needs with our wants. We get anxious when we think we have to follow the latest fashions, have the latest car, and indulge in a wide variety of foods. But these are wants, not needs. Studies have shown that when people are supplied with basic needs, they are actually happier than many who have far more than they need.

But God asks something of us if He is to supply all our needs, and that is to seek first His Kingdom. Put your love of God, prayer and following His direction first, then, the Scripture says, your needs will be provided.

Any experience in this? When you follow your own desires, wants, and plans for your life, leaving God out, where do you end up?

4. Matt. 14:22-33

Peter was so impressed with the Lord's feeding of the 5000 and His walking on water that he put his trust in Him and attempted to walk on the sea. He was able to do so as long as he maintained his trust and kept his eyes on the Lord. What happened when he looked at the waves tossed by the sea? He became afraid, began to sink, and cried out, "Lord! Save me!" And the Lord reached out His hand and caught him but reprimanded him for having little faith.

What is so beautiful about this passage is that the Lord commanded Peter to come when Peter asked, but even when Peter began to sink, the Lord rescued him. He supported Peter when Peter trusted him and rescued him when his faith failed.

We are urged to have faith, but God honors our weakness, and when we falter, He often rescues us. What is your experience in this?

Did God rescue you from something worse by allowing you to end up in jail?

5. Rom. 8:31-38

This should be the foundation and the grounding of our faith when it comes to trust. The love of God in Christ is beyond our understanding. That's why Paul has to list everything from death to all aspects of Creation to try to convince us there is nothing that can keep God from loving us. With such love, we can direct our soul, mind, heart, and body toward this reality so that whatever happens to us, even death, we are surrounded and encompassed by that incredible love.

We learn to trust God when we open ourselves to His love. By committing ourselves to that love and beginning to trust Him in every aspect of our lives, we, like Paul, become "more than conquerors through Him who loves us."

Read: Other Voices

SPIRITUAL GROWTH

Waiting for God

"They that wait upon the Lord, shall renew their strength." (Isaiah 40:31)

Lord, I'm so weary of waiting. Day in and day out with the same old grey walls to look at and friends turning on and off in their friendship. I'm becoming a different person here, and I believe it is because You are truly my only Friend. But I know You are my God, too, and can bring about changes in me that no one on earth can, including myself. I know I'm made in Your image and likeness, and my waiting here is helping to bring this about as I learn to pray more and more and stay in Your Word. Help me to see meaning in my waiting and to open my heart more and more to Your Presence, so that this time of waiting may be one of the best times of my life. In the name of the One who also waits for so many to come to Him, Amen.

VOICES FROM THE BIBLE

Read Psalm 62: 1-8. I wait for God.
For God alone my soul waits in silence.

1) Luke 1:1-22 — *Zechariah waits to be able to speak*
2) Luke 1:23-25 — *Elizabeth waits to get pregnant*
3) Luke 1:26-38 — *Gabriel waits for a response from Mary*
4) Luke 1:39-56 — *Mary and Elizabeth wait together*
5) Luke 2:1-20 — *Joseph and Mary wait for Jesus' birth*
6) Luke 2:22-35 — *Simeon waits for the "consolation of Israel"*
7) Luke 2:41-52 — *Jesus had to wait to be found by His parents*

OTHER VOICES

In the very fast-paced world in which we all now live; things are set up for maximum speed and efficiency. Fast food restaurants are a favorite for many people because they like to be able to go through a fast drive-thru and receive their order in a matter of minutes. Computers are now moving faster than ever before, and they are allowing news events to hit the screen right after the news has actually occurred. We are so used to everything moving at break-neck speed, that we then have a very hard time in adjusting to the slower ways that God will work things out in our life.
-Michael Bradley

Waiting certainly plays an enormous role in the unfolding story of God's relationship to man. It is God's oft-repeated way of teaching us that His power is real and that He can answer our prayers without interference and manipulation from us, but we have trouble getting our will, our time schedules out of the way. -Catherine Marshall

...the Lord seems constantly to use waiting as a tool for bringing us the very best of his gifts. He made the children of Israel wait generations for their freedom from slavery in Egypt. Because of their stubborn disobedience, they had to wait 40 years before they were ready to enter the Promised Land. Waiting was the keynote of the exile. The whole story of the Old Testament is the patient waiting for "the fullness of time" of the Saviour's birth. And after Jesus' Ascension, those gathered in the upper room had to wait a full ten days for the coming of the Holy Spirit.
-Catherine Marshall.

YOUR VOICE

1) *How do you spend your time when you are waiting changes in your circumstances?*
2) *Why do we have such a difficult time waiting?*
3) *What does our culture tell us about waiting?*
4) *What are some of the benefits of waiting?*
5) *Do you know someone with whom you can be comfortable while waiting?*
6) *Do we wait for God, or does God wait for us?*

COMMENTARY & DISCUSSION

Waiting for God

Introduction

A funny/tragic little play came out in the 1950's called "Waiting for Godot" by Samuel Beckett. The two main characters on a desolate stage discussed the fact that they were waiting for someone. They were apparently homeless and were visited by several other characters who talked to them or entertained them while they waited. A young boy came on the stage at the end of the first act and told them that Godot was not coming that day and to come back the next day. The second act was similar to the first except that the young boy came on at the end and said that Godot was coming tomorrow, but the play ends and Godot never comes.

There are many interpretations of this strange little play, but one could be that in our secular society in which the existence of God is essentially denied, waiting for some other god is futile because he/she/it is not going to show up.

But what profound joy and blessed relief it is that in the fullness of time, in the history of the world, when all mankind was living in darkness, the glorious, transcendent Creator of all, who holds the universe in His hands, wrapped Himself in the flesh of a little baby, came down to be with us, and ended our waiting.

We speak of the time before His birth as Advent, which means "to come," and we will look today at the people who were waiting for His birth. Then we will talk about what we do while we are waiting for the changes in our lives and how we can invite God to wait with us.

Read Psalm 62: 1-8

Sometimes when we believe God is absent and spend time waiting to hear His words to us, it may be that God is waiting for us—for further growth in our lives, for a deeper prayer life, or for a change in lifestyle. We need to be attentive to these areas if we expect God to speak to us and guide us. Sometimes He puts us on hold until we are ready to hear Him. The silence in the Psalms is essential, but it must be accompanied by having our lives in order in other ways.

Let's look at Luke 1-2 and learn from those waiting for the birth of Christ: What did they do while waiting?

1. Luke 1:1-22

Zechariah and Elizabeth had been married for many years and had no children. In the culture at that time, this was viewed with reproach. On one occasion while serving his turn at being a priest, an angel came to Zechariah and told him not to fear because Elizabeth will have a son who will announce the Kingdom of God and, in the spirit of Elijah, be a forerunner of the Messiah. But

Zechariah doubted what the angel said; thus he was made mute until the child was born. Not only did Zechariah and Elizabeth have to wait many years before having a child, but Zechariah had to wait for the son to be born before he could speak again.

2. Luke 1:23-25

Elizabeth conceived but did not feel her babe move until Mary (vs. 40) came to visit her in her third month, and when the babe heard the voice of the mother of his Lord, he leaped in her womb and made himself known. Elizabeth had to wait until the visitation of Mary before she could feel the babe in her womb.

3. Luke 1:26-38

Gabriel presented this great plan to Mary, telling her that God wanted her for a special task, and he persuaded her by describing that this Son would be great, the Son of the most High; He would be given the throne of David, would reign forever, and His Kingdom would have no end. Gabriel had to wait for Mary's response, answering the questions she posed.

4. Luke 1:39-56

Mary and Elizabeth wait together. This is when the babe, John, leaps for joy when he hears the voice of the mother of his Lord. Mary sings her famous song of the Magnificat, predicting the signs of the coming Kingdom of her Son: the great reversal when the rich shall be poor and the poor rich (in the ways of the Kingdom). She celebrates in advance what He will bring to the world. This song is sung in many churches even to this day.

5. Luke 2:1-20

Joseph and Mary wait for the coming of this special child. They travel to Bethlehem and wait in a cave because there was no other place for them to stay. The Babe is born there among the animals, and shepherds are the first to hear the good news and travel to Bethlehem to visit him.

6. Luke 2:22-35

Simeon waits for the "consolation of Israel." The prediction of a Messiah had been in Jewish tradition for a long time. This is the One Simeon has been longing to see, and God had assured him in some way that he would view this special Child before he departs. He finally views Him in Mary's arms. He also warned Mary that she would experience pain similar to a sword piercing her heart. She had to wait much longer before learning the meaning of that prophecy.

7. Luke 2:41-52

Joseph, Mary, and Jesus travel to Jerusalem for the yearly Passover. The boy Jesus remains behind. He waits for three days for His parents to return to find Him, meanwhile teaching the elders of the synagogue.

There are times of waiting in our lives: to get out of jail, for a new job, for a baby to be born, for reconciliation with estranged loved ones, etc. Henri Nouwen, in his essay "Waiting for God," advises us how we can wait, inviting God's presence as we do so.

1) Wait with expectancy. How do we wait with expectancy? Expect good at the end of your waiting. God is working in your life to bring about the best possible outcome. Don't be pessimistic, be positive. Anticipate a bright future.

2) Waiting is active, not passive. What should we be doing while we wait? Exploring options upon release from jail for jobs, furthering education, and getting in touch with family and friends.

3) Waiting involves patience. How can we practice patience while we wait? First, we can wait in the moment, practice silence and listening. This could be a time of learning more about yourself. Read for spiritual benefit. Consider how long a seed must stay in the ground before it can sprout.

4) Waiting is open ended. What does this mean? It can mean that we don't lock our expectations into one outcome. Someone said if you want to make God laugh, tell Him your plans. Be creative, open to what God sends you. Explore the many opportunities that might be available after you are released.

5) Wait together. How do we manage this? It is difficult to wait alone. Stay close to those who care for you. Make some new friends while you are here. They, too, are waiting and need companionship. Come to Bible studies to be with like-minded people who are on a spiritual journey.

6) Wait by listening to God. What are some of the ways you can do this? Primarily through church attendance, a regular prayer life, daily Scripture reading, and prayers for your own spiritual growth and the spiritual growth of others. And a major part of prayer is listening. Use the Centering Prayer guidelines to help you with this.

Read: Other Voices

Set your Heart on the Greatest Gift, Which is Love

God of surprises, You overwhelm us most with the depth, height, width and length of Your love for us. You came to earth, simply to show Your love to us. When we tortured and killed You, Your love had such great power that death could not hold You, so you arose from the grave and ascended into heaven. You continue to love us through Your Holy Spirit who dwells within our hearts. Help us to open fully to Your Spirit that we may be transformed by Your love into Your likeness. In the name of the Father, the Son and the Holy Spirit. Amen

VOICES FROM THE BIBLE

Read Psalm 18:1-19. The Lord delights in me!
He reached from on high, he took me, he drew me out of many waters.

1) Gen. 3:1-15 — *God's tough love to Adam and Eve*
2) Luke 6:32-36 — *Love your enemies*
3) Luke 10:25-37 — *And who is my neighbor?*
4) 1 John 3:11-24 — *Love in deed and in truth*
5) I Cor. 13 — *The greatest of these is love*

OTHER VOICES

Love breeds love. This is the only way that it spreads out into the world. In other words, in this world love is its own source. It cannot be reached through will or intellect or understanding. It springs out of the total reality of a human being—body, soul and mind—that has been touched directly by divine Love or from another person who has been touched by the Holy One and shares that love with us… One reason that the pagan world embraced Christianity was the love that Christians dying in the arena showed to one another and the pagans. Commenting on this, one scholar wrote that when modem Christians no longer show that kind of love, the world will become pagan again.
-Morton Kelsey

God is sufficiently wise, and good and powerful and merciful to tum even the most apparently disastrous events to the advantage and profit of those who humbly adore and accept his will in all that he permits. Let us be sure that God arranges all for the best. Our fears, our activities, our urgencies make us imagine inconveniences where in reality they do not exist. Let us leave all to God and then all will go well. Abandon to Him everything in general: that is the best way, indeed the only way of providing infallibly and surely for all our real interests.
-Jean Pierre de Caussade

God so loved the world ...For the exceeding great love God had towards us—when we had put ourselves far, far, far away from him and were trapped, morose, dying a dead death—He came to us, stooped to us, caught us up in the living heart of his Son, healed our crookedness, unwound our bonds, transformed our despair into joyful hope and praise.
-Ruth Burrows

From the first second of your existence, Love has been overflowing into you, growing you, mothering you, fathering you, delighting in you, never taking loving eyes away from you, whatever you did, however you behaved. And Love will continue this embrace into eternity... Love lives not only in you but in the persons next to you and in humanity half a globe away. Love brings you all together to create a single harmony, playing Its own love song from the depths of your innermost cells to the farthest reaches of the universe.
-Jane Marie Thibault

YOUR VOICE

1. *Someone said that anger and love are two sides of the same coin. How might this be true?*
2. *Describe an experience of God's love in your life.*
3. *Why is it impossible to love God and not neighbor, or to love neighbor and not God? Do you know of people who do one or the other?*
4. *Why is love both giving and receiving?*

Greek words for love: *storge* (affection), *philia* (brotherly love), *eros* (desire/sensual love), *agape* (sacrificial love).

COMMENTARY & DISCUSSION

Set Your Heart on the Greatest Gift, Which is Love

Introduction

What is the word that comes to mind when you see the way our culture defines the word "love"? Too often we think of it in connection with sex due to the many associations between the two on television and advertising. Further, we tend to sentimentalize the word by thinking of love as a "feeling," a strictly emotional state. Also, we exhaust the meaning of it by using it for expressions totally distinct from each other; for example, we say we love God and we love pizza. That really stretches the meaning of the word.

But in the original Greek of the New Testament there are four words for love. *Storge* means affection, as in "I *storge* my cat." *Philia* means brother love. The name "Philadelphia" is based on this word and means the city of brotherly love. *Eros* means desire and usually refers to sexual love, but someone can have an erotic love for God in the sense of desiring to know Him. And finally, *agape* means sacrificial love, which is what Jesus did on the cross and what you do for your children and others you love when you sacrifice for them. *Agape* is the only word for love that Jesus ever used in the New Testament.

Let's look at the Scriptures to see what they tell us about the meaning of that word for love.

Read Psalm 18:1-19

David had just been rescued from his enemies, namely Saul, who was, out of jealousy, attempting to kill him. He is expressing his gratitude for God's love and care for him. He is responding by expressing his love for God because God has delivered him. This Psalm also gives one of the most magnificent theophanies—God revealing himself—in the Old Testament in verses 6-19. God literally disrupts all of Creation to come down to save His servant David, who claims that God "delivered me because He delighted in me." Both God's power and His love are expressed to the utmost in this Psalm.

Should we love and praise God for only what He does for us? Why else should we love and praise him?

1. Gen. 3:1-15

This is the first example of tough love in human history. God loved Adam and Eve so much that he let them experience the result of their choices. He didn't just overlook their disobedience; He didn't just expel them from the Garden. They chose to be deprived of fellowship with Him because they wanted to do it their way. They broke the rules of the Garden and suffered the consequences.

God doesn't punish us when we make bad choices by doing wrong. He lets us experience the consequences of those choices. These can have devastating results for us. But only by experiencing the results of our sins can we hopefully learn that we must turn to God for guidance and walk in His way.

Do you see this as God exercising " tough love"?

But there's a hidden element in this Scripture that shows that even when we choose the way of destruction, as Adam and Eve did, God provides a way out.

God says to the snake: "There will be enmity between you and woman and between your offspring and hers; it will bruise your head (Christ will end your reign) and you (the devil) will strike its heel (have Him crucified)."

This is the first reference to the Messiah who will redeem Adam and Eve and all of humanity. And this is promised to Adam and Eve and to all of us on the very occasion of the Fall.

All of us have at some time turned our backs on God and tried to follow our own misguided desires and goals, yet God provides a way out. He comes down to earth in the form of His Son and allows the serpent to strike His heel (the Crucifixion), but his Son will strike the head of the snake, the instrument of death, by conquering death through His Resurrection.

How often do you succeed by mapping out your own path and ignoring the guidance and the way of the Lord? Do you learn from the consequences of bad choices?

2. Luke 6:32-36

Too often our own worst enemy is ourselves. Love yourself because God loves you. You are lovable. He delights in you. You can only love your enemies if you accept God's love for you.

Do you really love yourself? What does it mean to love yourself? How do you treat yourself when you love yourself? If you are good to yourself and care for yourself, is it easier to be kind to and to care for others? We can only truly love ourselves if we accept God's love of us.

His love shows us we are lovable, and by receiving His love, we then have the power to love others. We can love with the love with which we have been loved.

3. Luke 10:25-37

A lawyer comes to Jesus to test him and asks what he must do to inherit eternal life. Jesus asks him, "What does the Law say?" The lawyer replies, "You must love the Lord your God with all your heart, soul, strength and mind, and your neighbor as yourself." Jesus commends him for answering rightly. The lawyer then, goes on to ask, "Who is my neighbor?" and Jesus then tells the parable of the Good Samaritan.

A man is going on a journey down from Jerusalem to Jericho, a treacherous journey in those days. He is robbed, beaten, and left half dead. A priest and a Levite pass by, not touching him for fear he is dead, believing they would be made ritually impure if they touched him.

A Samaritan—a mixed breed of people hated by the Jews—sees the man, stops, anoints him with oil and wine (medicine in those days) puts him on his own beast and takes him to the nearest inn and leaves him. He promises more money when he returns, if that is necessary.

There is a lot to see in this passage. Some see Jesus as the Good Samaritan, who anoints the wounded man with (holy) oil, gives him the wine of the Eucharist, and takes him to the Church.

But we want to look at the parable in terms of loving the neighbor. What does the parable tell us about who our neighbor is? The neighbor is the one in need. How can we recognize the needy neighbor? With some needs it is obvious: food, clothing, housing, a job. But the emotional and spiritual needs are not so easy to discern and sometimes can be more devastating.

Also, some false "charity" may not involve love but can rather be an attempt to bring glory to oneself. Some "charity" can be done with a bad attitude: "just doing my duty, getting it out of the way."

Real love has empathy for the neighbor, opens one heart to the neighbor, and is with him in his pain and suffering.

What neighbor have you ministered to lately? And how did you do it?

4. I John 3:11-24

A sign that we have passed from death to life is that we love our brothers and sisters. We cannot love in a mature and responsible way unless we are open to receiving God's love, which enables us to love ourselves. Jesus said, "Love your neighbor as you love yourself." There is no way we can love others if we hate ourselves. We will just project our self-hatred on to other people. And the only way we can love ourselves is by being constantly open to God's love for us through prayer, Bible Study and worship.

John goes on to say that hating someone is equal to murder. Where does murder begin? In the heart of the murderer. Jesus reminds us in the Sermon on the Mount that the seed of evil in within us. That's why we pray to have the Holy Spirit in our hearts: so that love reigns and not hatred.

Further, our love must not just be words but deeds. Love is a verb, not a squishy, sentimental feeling or an emotion. Love acts, as we will see in our next Scripture.

5. I Cor. 13:1-12

I've given you a handout of a contemporary translation of I Cor. 13 because it tells us what love is in language we are very familiar with. I'll read, and you follow along on the handout, then we will discuss it.

J.D. Pedersen's *The Message*:

"If I speak with human eloquence and angelic ecstasy but don't love, I'm nothing but the creaking of a rusty gate. If I speak God's Word with power, revealing all his mysteries and making everything plain as day, and if l have faith that says to a mountain: "Jump" and it jumps, but I don't love, I'm nothing. If I give everything I own to the poor and even go to the stake to be burned as a martyr, but I don't love, I've gotten nowhere. So, no matter what I say, what I believe, and what I do, I'm bankrupt without love. Love never gives up. Love cares more for others than for self. Love doesn't want what it doesn't have. Love doesn't strut, Doesn't have a swelled head, Doesn't force itself on others, Isn't always "me first," Doesn't fly off the handle, Doesn't keep score of the sins of others, Doesn't revel when others grovel, Takes pleasure in the flowering of truth, Puts up with anything, Trusts God always, Always looks for the best, Never looks back, But keeps going to the end. Love never dies. Inspired speech will be over some day; praying in tongues will end; understanding will reach its limit. We know only a portion of the truth, and what we say about God is always incomplete. But when the Complete arrives, our incompletes will be canceled… But right now, until that Completeness comes, we have three things to do to lead us toward that consummation: Trust steadily in God; hope unswervingly, love extravagantly, and the best of these three is love."

Are any of these characteristics of love about "feeling" or emotions?

No, they are all about the way we behave toward others and about humility, patience, perseverance, and trust.

But how many of us can always love in this way? None of us. That's why Christ sent the Holy Spirit to help us love, to help us understand what love is, and to recognize when and how we need to exercise it toward others.

What will you do to become more loving toward God and toward others?

Read: Other Voices

Dear Christ, We are Called to Be Like You!

Gracious and glorious God, we read of Your Transfiguration in the Gospel and know this is what we are called to become. We aren't just saved FROM something, we are saved TO something and that something is to become like You, to live with You eternally in the Kingdom of Love. And we know, with Your help, we can begin on this earth to become like You. Help us to focus on Your love for us, that love which can transfigure us into Your likeness as we go through our daily life. Your healing power is available to us today as well as forever. Help us to open ourselves to it. Amen.

VOICES FROM THE BIBLE

Read Psalm 27. Wait for the Lord!
Thy face, Lord, do I seek. Hide not thy face from me.

1) Exodus 24:12-18, 34:29-35 — *Moses beholds the glory of the Lord*
2) Matt. 17:1-9 — *The Lord was transfigured on the mountain*
3) Col. 1:15-23 — *He will present you holy and blameless*
4) II Cor. 3:12-18 — *We are being changed into His likeness*
5) Phil. 3:12-16 — *Our lowly bodies will become like His*
6) II Peter 1:1-20 — *The morning star will rise in your hearts*

OTHER VOICES

Glory is the song which sings from the words of the Gospel; it is the flame that springs up within me when the word touches my heart. And it is God—excess, pure gratuity, transcendent in Being—who is more intimate to me than my own hungry and struggling self. Glory is that which glows at the extremes of experience, at the heights and the depths of life. Everything in the world moves toward glory as its flowering, its coming to flame, its truth. Shame is the inverse of glory, a terrible knowledge of our destiny, the awful nakedness we feel without the garment of Light. Beauty is the icon of glory, the light of eternity on the features of time.
-M. M. Funk

Our submission to the salvation of Christ is a submission of our life to the life of grace—a recognition that there is no salvation apart from Christ and the life of grace. In cultural terms, it means a renunciation of the secular life—a life defined by my needs as a consumer within the modern experience—and an acceptance of my life as defined by the Cross of Christ. If the Cross is to be taken up with integrity—it must be taken up daily. The life of grace means that I have given myself to Christ and to the means He has provided for my salvation. I will confess my sins and embrace the life of repentance. I will approach the Cup of His Body and Blood with faith and with trust in His promise of Life. I will be patient as I await His coming to me, as forgiveness, as healing, as transformation from the death of Adam into the Life of Christ. All of which requires that we "show up"—not in the casual sense of the term but in the sense that we truly struggle to make

ourselves available to God. How shall we escape if we neglect so great a salvation? (Hebrews 2:3)
-Stephen Freeman

We must always pray the Lord for peace of soul that we may the more easily fulfill the Lord's commandments, for the Lord loves those who strive to do His will, and thus they attain profound peace in God. He who does the Lord's will is content with all things, though he be poor or sick and suffering, because the grace of God gladdens his heart. But the man who is discontented with his lot and murmurs against his fate, or against those who cause him offense, should realize that his spirit is in a state of pride, which has taken from him his sense of gratitude towards God. But if it be so with you, do not lose heart, but try to trust firmly in the Lord and ask Him for a humble spirit, and when the lowly Spirit of God comes to you, you will then love Him and be at rest in spite of all tribulations. The soul that has acquired humility is always mindful of God and thinks to herself: "God has created me. He suffered for me. He forgives me my sins and comforts me. He feeds me and cares for me. Why, then should I take thought for myself, and what is there to fear, even if death threaten me?"
-Staretz Silouan

YOUR VOICE

1) *Can you see your own Christian growth as becoming like Christ?*
2) *What does it mean to lose the way on your journey to God? How does this affect the way you live?*
3) *What does repentance ("metanoia"—turning in the other direction) have to do with Christian growth? Is this a one-time event?*
4) *What are some of the characteristics of being "God-like"?*
5) *What does being God-like have to do with our relationships with others?*

COMMENTARY & DISCUSSION

Dear Christ, We are Called to Be Like You!

Introduction

The main teaching of Christianity is that we are called to become like Christ and since God is in Christ, we are called to become God-like. The word for this is "deification" (God (deity)-like). An early saint whose name was St. Athanasius said that "God became man, that man might become like God." That's our *telos* (goal, destination): to become like God. We become by grace what God is by nature. It's like a sword in a fire. A steel sword thrust into a fire turns red hot. It doesn't become the fire, but it glows with the light and the heat of the fire. We are little swords, and thrust into the fire and light of Christ, we take on His glow.

In Creation, we were made in the image and likeness of God. We bear His image at birth, forever stamped with it. However, through sin, we become distorted and we can only grow into His likeness by His grace and with our cooperation through the Church, prayer, Bible study, a Christian lifestyle, and showing love to our brothers and sisters.

When Christ took on flesh and became a human being, He began the process by which we can be renewed as we are joined to Him. By baptism, we begin to be recreated in His image. We can stumble, fall, and retreat into sin, but we can always repent and return to Him and to continue our growth into His likeness.

This is our destiny as Christians, to become Christ-like. This is where we are heading if we stay close to God with devotion to Him and His will. God is not just going to scoop us up and re-create us in His image. If we truly claim to be Christians, we have our role to play. Paul says, "Work out your own salvation with fear and trembling." (Phil.2:12) We are co-creators with God in transforming us into His likeness. This is what salvation is.

Read Psalm 27:4-14

Vs. 4 says we want to dwell in His house and behold His beauty. We become like what we look at. If you look at TV all the time, especially the ads, you are going to adopt the values that TV teaches which are: me first, pleasure above all, consume all you can, etc. What are some other messages from TV? (violence, sex, religious heresies, etc.)

Vs. 8: Seek ye my face. The Orthodox church has icons, images of what they believe Christ looked like. But you can look at His face with your spiritual eyes and see His kindness, His holiness, His compassion, His suffering. When we look at Christ, we can see what we will become. The face of God on this earth is the face of Jesus Christ.

Vs. 9: We ask the Lord not to hide His face from us, but when we turn away from Him in sin, we become blind to His beauty and love.

Vs. 10: Even though our father and mother forsake us, the Lord will take us up. This has to be a comfort when we are at times so alienated from family and other kin.

Vs. 14: What does "wait" for the Lord mean? It can mean a focus on Him through prayer, devotion and worship. Maybe only when we "wait" for the Lord can our faith increase by trusting Him with what is coming our way.

1. Ex. 24:12-18; 34:29-35

Moses, the Israelite chosen by God to bring His people to the Promised land, not only led them out of Egypt and into the Wilderness but was the one whom God called to ascend Mt. Sinai and receive the Law. Moses had to be separated from his people in order to come into communion, into conversation with God. He stayed on the mountain for 40 days, during which time a cloud descended and covered him while he received what God chose to give him.

What other Biblical events took 40 days? (Israelites in the wilderness, Jesus tempted in the desert, rain on Noah's ark for 40 days and 40 nights, etc.)

During the 40 days while Moses was on Mt. Sinai, the Israelites became impatient, believing that Moses and God had forsaken them. They talked Aaron into building a false god, a golden calf from all their jewelry. When Moses came down, he was so angry that he broke the tablets on which were written the law and commandments.

God commanded Moses to return to the mountain so He could restore the tablets, and when Moses came down this time, his face shone so brightly, reflecting the glory of the Lord, he had to put a veil over it. His encounter with the Holy God transformed his face, reflecting God's glory.

In the Scriptures, a mountain is quite often a place of revelation where people meet God. Many monasteries are built on mountains to enable the monks not to be distracted by others and to spend time in prayer and contemplation to grow closer to God.

We talk about a "mountain-top experience" as a deep and profound spiritual experience that brings us closer to God and can begin to transform us.

Have you ever had a "mountain-top" experience?

Moses' experience on Mt. Sinai was a foreshadowing of the Lord's experience on Mt. Tabor, which we will read next. Moses was also at this mountain-top event.

2. Matt. 17:1-9

The Lord was transfigured on Mt. Tabor before his disciples. What is similar in this passage to the Moses story?

On Mt. Tabor, a bright cloud descended on Christ as a cloud descended on Moses on Mt Sinai.

On Mt. Tabor, only holy people were there: Christ, Elijah and Moses (the three disciples who were there fell over in awe of the transformed Christ). Moses was accompanied by Joshua on Mt. Sinai, but only Moses entered the cloud with God.

The garments and the face of Christ shone like the sun on Tabor, and Moses' face shone when he came down the mountain the second time.

The voice of God at the Transfiguration spoke: "This is my Beloved Son, hear Him;" the voice of God on Sinai gave the Law to Moses.

What The Transfiguration shows to His disciples is Christ's divinity, so that when He was crucified, His disciples would not despair but would remember that they saw Him in His full glory transfigured on the mountain.

On Mt. Tabor, Moses represents the law and all who have died. Elijah represents the prophets and, since he did not experience death but went up to heaven in a whirlwind, represents all those who are alive in Christ. Further, it shows that the law and the prophets bear witness to Jesus as the Messiah and the fulfillment of the Old Testament law and prophets.

Why did the disciples fall on their faces? This was similar to the time the Israelites were overwhelmed by the glory shown on Moses' face.

Christ's transformed image on Mt. Tabor is a prediction of our own eventual transformation in Christ.

How overwhelming is this? Is there any other source in our culture today that provides such affirmation of who we are and our destiny as Christians?

3. Col. 1:15-23

This passage is an ancient Christian hymn that Paul uses to voice his theology. There are two parts to it. The first states that Christ is the Head of Creation. The early Christian creeds claim that all things were made by Him. The second part of the hymn states that Christ is the founder of the new creation, which resulted in the salvation of the world due to His death and resurrection.

Christ is both God and Man, and as the image of man, He is the firstborn of the new creation, and we will follow Him into God's Kingdom as we are transformed into His likeness.

How do we begin this transformation into His likeness while we are here on earth?

4. II Cor. 3:12-18

Moses had to put a veil over his face, because it shone so brightly from being with God on Mt. Sinai when he received the Ten Commandments. If the people had looked at his face reflecting God's glory, they would have been overwhelmed.

Paul says the Jews still fail to accept the truth of Christ the Messiah of the New Testament and thus still have a veil covering their faces.

But when we turn to the Lord, says Paul, the veil is taken away, and through faith we see the glory of the Lord. As we look at Him through prayer, church, worship and obedience, we are being changed from glory into glory into His image.

5. Phil. 3: 12-16

Paul is turning his back on the evils he did in his life—persecuting Christians, sanctioning the martyrdom of Stephen—and is pressing upward toward the goal of becoming like Christ. He asks that we be of the same mind.

To imitate him we must turn our back on our sinful past; we must reject the temptations of the world and disdain an ungodly lifestyle; we must not live solely for material things and the values of the world. He especially mentions obsession with food, which is characteristic of our contemporary culture.

We are citizens of another city, which is Heaven, for which we wait for Jesus Christ who will transform our bodies into the likeness of His Body.

We can look back at the Transfiguration and see what we will become when we become like Christ.

How hard is it for you to forget the past? How difficult is to believe you will have a glorious Christ-like body when we are united with Christ in glory?

6. II Peter 1:1-20

Peter urges us, since we are becoming like Christ, to manifest these qualities in our lives: virtue, knowledge, self-control, perseverance, and Godliness. How can you while incarcerated begin the practice of these qualities?

- Virtue - make the attempt to be honest and kind.
- Knowledge - attend Bible study; read Scripture and good books on your own.
- Self-control - resolve to break your addictions (with help) and move on.
- Perseverance - "do the time, don't let the time do you." Don't have a victim mentality; look to the future and make plans for your release.
- Godliness - act like Christ: be kind, truthful, compassionate, and show love to all.

Peter goes on to say he is not just making up this experience, devising some sort of new age stuff or tale, but that the disciples actually saw the Lord in all His glory on the holy mountain (Mt. Tabor) and heard the Father say, "This is my beloved Son, in whom I am well pleased. Hear Him."

Peter goes to say, "Heed this as a light that shines in a dark place until the morning star rises in your hearts," referring to Christ's return.

This is the hope we have and on which we focus—our own transformation—as we are changed from glory unto glory by a devout life of prayer, worship, good deeds, and following and imitating Christ.

Read: Other Voices

Dear God, Free Me From the Idolatry of Addiction

"Whatever we are ultimately concerned with is god for us." -Paul Tillich

Dear Father: The addiction in my life can be an easy substitute for facing myself and opening up to Your love. Whether it is a chemical or a behavioral addiction, it means I am running away from You toward disaster. Please help me by sending your Holy Spirit to open me up to that love that can give me the courage to face myself, to see my worth as a person and to walk in the path which You have for me. And send me the friends, the supports, the helps I need to get me on Your straight and narrow way that leads to wholeness and peace. In the name of the One who is with me on every step of the journey, your precious Son, Jesus Christ. Amen.

VOICES FROM THE BIBLE

Isaiah 61:1-4. He comforts the afflicted.
He has sent me to proclaim liberty to the captives and the opening of the prison to those who are bound.

1) 1 John 1:5-10   *If we walk in darkness*
2) Rom. 6:12-19   *Yield yourselves to God*
3) I Cor. 6:15-20   *Your body is a temple*
4) James 1:12-14   *God tempts no one*
5) Phil. 2:5-11   *He took the form of a slave*
6) Rom. 8:31-39   *Nothing can separate us from Christ's love*

OTHER VOICES

God's love is unconditional, eternal, merciful, unchanging, vulnerable, sacrificial and unquenchable. God's love leads us Home. The great gift of our addiction is the opportunity to know—really know—that you are desperate for Love, to give up on yourself and to give in to Another. Take to heart the words of the apostle John. Let these words become your home when you are tempted to wander, or when you get lost again along the way: "What marvelous love the Father has extended to us! Just look at it—we're called children of God! That's who we really are." (I John 3:1) Don't stop looking for or looking at His love. Giving in to Him is the last answer to the last addiction which is believing you can heal yourself.
-Sharon Hersh

Some of our stories describe abandonment, betrayal, and ambivalence. We experience those losses and assaults as orphans, strangers, and widows. Should it surprise us then, that God wants to make Himself known as the Father who protects the orphans, as the Brother who encourages the strangers, and as the Lover who cherishes the widows? The Triune God who is One wants to redeem our story and restore with His love what our story took from us.
-Dan Allender

We are waiting for the day when we are really home and all things are new. Waiting is hard, scary, risky, humbling, and may be embarrassing. We have days of great joy and days of great struggle. We rely on ourselves and remember that we need God. We live like exiles and find others to walk with us along the Way. We are enticed by the promises of this world and long for the promises of a world to come. We take two steps forward and three steps back. But if we will just give in and be quiet for a few minutes, we can hear God's whisper: *This is how I am making all things new.*
-Sharon Hersh

YOUR VOICE

1) We live in a society of addicts. Why is this so? How many types of addiction can you identify?
2) What are some of the events and experiences that provoke us into addiction, of any type?
3) Can you grow spiritually while you are in some sort of addiction? Why or why not?
4) What can the Church do to help addicts?
5) Do you know of other sources of healing besides the Church and Twelve Steps?
6) Why is addiction a form of idolatry?

Sharon Hersh's book, *The Last Addiction: Why Self-Help is Not Enough*, is highly recommended for anyone struggling with addiction or with an addicted loved one.

COMMENTARY & DISCUSSION

God, Free me From the Idolatry of Addiction

Introduction

Isaiah says in 2:8: "Their land is full of idols." That is what addiction is—it is worship of something/someone other than the true God. When anything—a person, a place, a substance, an activity, or some sort of political belief—becomes the main focus of your mind, soul and spirit, it is an addiction and literally becomes the god you worship. It can be anything from alcohol to religious activity. When it begins to interact with all aspects of your life, it is an addiction. The root of the word addiction gives us an insight into its nature. The Latin word "addictus" means "surrender to the gods."

There are several other ways of looking at addiction:

- I am not o.k. the way I am.
- There is a void that needs to be filled.
- There is something or someone external to myself that will fill this void.
- My happiness is dependent or finding this substance, possession, person or activity.
- Addiction is a flight from truth or a substitute for the truth.
- Recovery is a journey back to the truth. And who is the Way, the Truth and the Life? Only Jesus Christ.

One of the most effective ways of addressing substance addiction is through the Twelve Steps of Alcoholics Anonymous and other similar programs. Many people are familiar with these steps and have used them. The reason they work so well is that they are based on the truths of Scripture: recognizing that one is powerless over one's addiction, the need to surrender to a higher Power, admitting wrongs, asking forgiveness, improving one's relationship with God as He is understood, and carrying the message to others. Oddly, they do not mention in the Twelve Steps the need for community, which is absolutely essential and is met by attending AA meetings.

However, the foremost source for community and healing must be the Church with accompanying prayer, Bible study, and spiritual direction. The Twelve Steps program simply puts in other words the spiritual healing offered by the Church.

How can Scripture help us to understand addiction and how healing can take place?

Read Isaiah 61:1-4

This passage identifies the Source of our healing. When Jesus gave His first sermon in His hometown of Nazareth, He identified characteristics similar to those of the addicted and stated His mission to heal them:

"The Spirit of the Lord is upon me for God has anointed me. He has sent me to bring the good news to the afflicted, to soothe the broken hearted, to proclaim liberty to the captives, to release to those in prison."

Each of these conditions could apply to one who is addicted. Release from affliction, brokenhearted, captive, imprisonment. Physical jail is paradise compared to being a soul in the prison of addiction. Paul summed it up in Romans 7:19, which could be a description of uncontrollable addiction: "For I do not do the good I want, but the evil I do not want is what I do."

And the Messiah, the Anointed one, is the ultimate source of all of our healing. What are your observations or experiences of addiction?

1. 1 John 1:5-10

If we claim to have fellowship with Him and walk in darkness, we lie and do not practice the truth. This is one who is in denial. Addiction puts us in darkness, and to claim we are in the light when we are not is denial, the basic characteristic of the addicted person. All addicts are in denial. Have you ever tried to tell an alcoholic not to drink, a dope addict not to use, a compulsive shopper to stay home, a sex addict to restrain themselves?

We cannot begin the healing process until we come out of denial and admit we have a problem and are powerless to solve it. How do we come out of denial? Usually some catastrophe has to happen to bring this about: arrest, a spouse leaving, children acting out, a health crisis, an intervention. To wait for someone to hit bottom quite often doesn't do it. The person just gets up and continues in their addiction.

John goes on to say that when we begin to walk in the light as He is in the light, then we can have fellowship with each other. There is no fellowship with one who is addicted.

Why is this so?

2. Rom. 6:12-19

You can substitute "addiction" for "sin" in this text for the purposes of this study. However, not all sin is addictive, but all addiction is sin because it is idolatry. From one point of view, we are all addicts when we give our ultimate loyalty to something or someone instead of God.

If sin reigns or rules your body as Paul says, you are a slave to it. If you indulge in the addiction, you are a slave to it.

To be freed from slavery to addiction, by God's grace through Jesus Christ, you become a slave to righteousness with worship of the one true God.

3. I Cor. 6:15-20

"'Prostitute" might be a word for those on chemical addiction. Will you turn your body over to a substance that destroys body, soul, mind and spirit? You are selling your body to a substance that can maim or kill you and that destroys your relationship with others.

Behavioral addiction does not destroy the body (unless you have to have knee replacement from walking the mall shopping!) However, it too can greatly compromise our relationships with others. Chemical or ingested addiction does destroy the body. There is a brain disorder, Korsakoff's syndrome, which causes chronic memory disorder, which is a direct result of over-consumption of alcohol

Our bodies are temples, sacred, holy, made in the image and likeness of God. Do you realize how incredibly expensive we are, what it cost God to bring us home?

4. James 1:12-14

The addicted person never refuses temptation. They are constantly yielding. It takes major work and constant surrender to God to break this cycle. James warns you to stay on the straight and narrow when you are freed from addiction. Don't blame God when you are tempted to succumb again to whatever addiction you may have had.

Staying on the path requires that you be in touch with a community. Twelve Steps doesn't mention the importance of this, but they practice it because they know how important it is. AA groups, or some supportive community, are essential to staying sober, and they make a point to their participants that they must "work the program," or in 90 days from their last drink, they will " fall off the wagon" and resume their addiction.

Sharon Hersh says: "If you feel stuck in your recovery from addiction, mired down in an exhausting determination to be 'good,' feeling deflated and distant from God, I want to encourage you to stay on your tiptoes, looking with a steady gaze on the One who is Other, how we need Him—One who is eternal when we feel bogged down in time, One who is love when we are filled with self-contempt, One who is powerful when we feel impotent, One who is forgiveness when we feel unforgivable."

Why doesn't the Twelve Steps program alone heal our addiction?

5. Phil. 2:5-11

This passage is the heart of the Gospel, and the wording was a hymn in the early Christian community.

Our God is not one who sits in the heaven, watching us mess up time and time again. He humbled Himself, came down and became a criminal, involved Himself in our mess and took it on Himself.

He allowed Himself to be tortured and killed and overcame death by His Resurrection to free us from the results of our sin, our death, and our addictions.

Brennan Manning says, "He came to us not with the crushing impact of unbearable glory but in the way of weakness, vulnerability and need. Jesus was a naked, mutilated exposed God on the cross who allowed us to get close to him. At the cross, the very first became last, that we might be first. The winner became the loser, so that losers could become winners. At the cross, Jesus revealed the glory of God—love, mercy and unquenchable grace."

Sharon Hersh: "I can accept being a loser when I understand how God wins. He wins by losing. The apostle Paul explains it this way: "Though He was rich, yet for your sakes He became poor, so that you through His poverty might become rich." (II Cor. 8:9) That's the pattern we have to follow—*kenosis*—we descend into the darkness of facing who we are, and through Christ allow that person to die so that we can be brought to new life in Him."

Why must we lose our life in order to find it?

6. Rom. 8:31-39

This is the glorious statement by Paul of God's unrelenting, unfathomable, overwhelming, redeeming love. And the reality of it is that we don't discover this by searching for God, we accept it as God searching for us. His emptying of Himself, and being a part of our pain, suffering, our near destruction is the very means He uses to bring us back to Himself. "For I am sure that neither death, nor life, nor angels, nor principalities, nor things present, nor things to come, nor powers, not height nor depth, nor anything else in all creation, will be able to separate us from the love of God in Christ Jesus our Lord."

Not even addiction.

Read: Other Voices

The substance of this lesson was drawn from *The Last Addiction: Why Self-Help is Not Enough*, Sharon A. Hersh, Waterbrook Press, Colorado Springs, CO, 2008.

Dear God, Fill My Empty Heart with the Fruits of the Spirit

O Heavenly King, the Comforter, the Spirit of Truth, who art everywhere and fillest all things; Treasure of blessings and Giver of life, come and abide in us, cleanse us from every impurity and save our souls O Good One.

VOICES FROM THE BIBLE

Read Galatians 5:22. The fruits of the Spirit
…love, joy, peace, longsuffering, kindness, goodness, faithfulness, gentleness, self-control.

1)	I Cor.13	*And the greatest of these is love*
2)	James 1:2-8	*Count it all joy*
3)	John 14:25-31	*Peace I leave with you*
4)	Ps. 40:1-3	*Wait for the Lord*
5)	II Peter 1:5-9	*Have gentle care for others*
6)	Matt. 5:43-48	*Goodness is God-like*
7)	Heb. 11:1-3	*Faith and hope keep us going*
8)	Luke 10:29-37	*The good and gentle neighbor*
9)	Prov. 25:28	*Refrain from evil*

OTHER VOICES

"Love never fails." What a wonderful phrase that is! But what a still more wonderful thing the reality of that love: greater than prophecy—that vast forth-telling of the mind and purpose of God; greater than the practical faith that can remove mountains; greater than philanthropic self-sacrifice; greater than the extraordinary gift of emotions and ecstasies and all eloquence; and it is this love that is shed abroad in our hearts by the Holy Spirit which is given unto us.
-Beth Moore

The joy of the Lord is our strength. What a needed commodity! What a source of attractiveness to a broken and needy world! What a necessary fruit the Christian should make manifest. A philosopher of the 19th century said of Christians, "They have no joy." What a terrible judgment! Joy is the second characteristic of the fruit of the Spirit. Only love better describes the lifestyle of Christ. Only love more aptly meets the needs of our torrid age. Love melts the heart of stone. Joy touches the deepest part of that heart. We need joy, and our world needs believers who evidence the fruit of joy.
-Beth Moore

Faith. Many people struggle continually to have more of it. They groan and they strain like a woman in labor. They think: "If only I had more faith my prayers could be answered." Have you ever considered the relationship between faith and faithfulness? Faith is not an action; it is a response. If we strive to have faith, we may be miserably disappointed. But if we learn to trust in His faithfulness, we of all persons may be more blessed. As we revel in His faithfulness we will grow and develop in our own. -Beth Moore

The Greek word translated "fruit" refers to the natural product of a living thing. Paul used "fruit" to help us understand the product of the Holy Spirit, who lives in every Christian. The fruit of the Spirit is produced by the Spirit, not by the Christian. The Greek word is singular, showing that "fruit" is a unified whole, not independent characteristics. As we grow, all the characteristics of Christ will be manifested in our lives. Yet, like physical fruit needs time to grow, the fruit of the Spirit will not ripen in our lives overnight. Like a successful gardener must battle against weeds to enjoy the sweet fruit they desire, we must constantly work to rid our lives of the "weeds" of our sinful natures that want to choke out the work of the Spirit.
-Kathy Howard

YOUR VOICE

1) *Which "fruit" are you strongest in? Which are you weakest in?*
2) *What tools do you have/need to strengthen the weak ones?*
3) *Why might "love" be the first fruit mentioned? Should that be the one addressed first?*
4) *Why should developing all and not just one of the "fruits" be essential for an authentic and dedicated Christian life?*

COMMENTARY & DISCUSSION

Dear God, Fill my Empty Heart with the Fruits of the Spirit

To Instructor: Copy the bookmark page "Fruits of the Spirit" (See Appendix). Give one to each participant. Instruct them to keep the bookmark in their Bible and read it each day.

Introduction

Being filled with the Spirit is our goal as Christians. This describes the Christ, who was a perfect embodiment of these "fruits" and Who we are all called to imitate. Certainly, we will never be perfected on this earth, but these are the virtues we need to strive for in our Christian journey.

When you read your Bible each day, look at these "fruits" listed on your bookmark. Ask yourself: "How close am I coming to practicing these 'fruits'? Which ones do I need to work on?" Try concentrating on one each day. For example, today I'll be more loving or more joyful. Today I'll practice more self-control, etc.

Salvation is not a onetime fix. It is a journey. It will take time and lots of prayer to let the fruits fully mature in your heart. When you are baptized into Christ, the work is just beginning, but be assured Christ is walking with you and guiding you every step of the way.

Pray together: "O Heavenly King."

1. LOVE - I Cor. 13 - *The greatest of these is love*

You can do all sorts of good works without having a loving heart. And it will be wasted in terms of your own growth in God. Someone said, "You can be religious and still be lost." You can observe all the external rituals, but if you don't have true compassion and empathy for others grounded in a love for Christ, it amounts to nothing.

Love is misunderstood in our culture, partly because we use the same word for many different purposes. e.g. I love God and I love pizza. The Greeks had four words, *storge, philia, eros* and *agape*. *Agape* is the only word Jesus uses when He speaks of it in His ministry.

We also sentimentalize it by associating it with a feeling. Love is not a feeling. It is a form of behavior. It is a way of acting toward others and relating to them by putting their needs above your own. Jesus on the cross is the perfect embodiment of *agape* love.

2. JOY - James 1:2-8 - *Have joy, even in trials*

How can this be? Because for those who love God, all things work together for good, and we can believe that in all that we are going through, God is working through it for our salvation. Thus, true joy comes from knowing God is in control of everything and will make all things right someday. Paul gives us instructions on how to live and couples joy with prayer and thanksgiving. "Rejoice always, pray without ceasing and be thankful in all things." (1 Thess. 5:16-18)

3. PEACE - John 14:25-31 - *The peace that Christ gives*

The word "Counselor" refers back to the prayer to the Holy Spirit that we just prayed. The Counselor (Holy Spirit) teaches us and reminds us of what Christ wants us to know and become. The peace of Christ is not what the world gives. The world gives peace only when the events in our lives are going along well.

How often is this? Not very often. But the peace Christ gives transcends the circumstances of our lives and enables us to see them in a different light—the Light of Christ!

Christ is warning His disciples not to be afraid or troubled by His leaving them soon, for He will see them again after the Resurrection. His word to them at every encounter was the word, "peace." Jesus rising from the dead brings all of us to peace, because He has conquered death.

What do we often turn to if we cannot find inner peace? Usually some sort of addiction.

4. LONGSUFFERING - Psalms 40:1-3 - *Wait for the Lord*

Another word for longsuffering is "patience." The Psalmist waits patiently for the Lord, believing that the Lord has heard his cry and the Lord responds by bringing him out of the miry pit, setting his feet on a rock and putting a new song in his mouth.

Have you been rewarded in such a way when you have patiently waited for some answer to prayer? How difficult is it to wait, to be long suffering?

5. KINDNESS - II Peter 1:5-9 - *Add to your faith, kindness*

Peter adds kindness to the list of virtues that characterize true faith. Kindness means gentle concern and respect toward others. This can only happen if we can open ourselves to Christ's love and follow His way of life in which He was gentle and humble toward all.

6. GOODNESS - Matt 5:43-48 - *Do good to those who hate you*

The root word for "good" is God. So to be good means to be like God, who in Christ on the Cross forgave even those who crucified Him. We certainly can't attain that goal on this earth, but the Christian tradition teaches us that being like Christ is what we are called to be. Paul says we are being changed from glory unto glory to become like God. The word for that is "deification" which means God-like.

7. FAITHFULNESS - Heb. 11:1-3 - *Faith and hope keep us going*

The three characteristics that abide, as Paul says, are faith, hope and love. The greatest of these is love, the only one which will remain with us throughout eternity. Faith is the vessel which keeps us afloat on the deep, stormy sea of this life. How can we nurture this faith? By always keeping our eyes on Christ through prayer, Bible study, attending Church, and love toward others.

Do you have difficulty maintaining your faith? What helps do you turn to?

8. GENTLENESS - Luke 10:29-37 - *The good and gentle neighbor*

One of the most compassionate and gentle of Jesus' characters in any of His parables is the good Samaritan. In that parable, when both the priest and the Levite saw the wounded man, they moved to the other side of the road, fearing ritual uncleanliness if the man were dead. But the Samaritan, one of a group of people hated by the Jews because they had intermarried with foreigners, was the one who stopped and ministered to the victim. He even carried him to the inn and left money if it were needed for his further care.

Our culture today is not characterized very often by gentleness but rather harshness, aggressiveness, and lack of pity.

How do you express gentleness in your life?

9. SELF-CONTROL - Prov. 25:28 - *Refrain from evil*

A city without walls is one in which anyone can enter. This virtue requires a lot of discipline. The root word of discipline is "disciple." Our minds, if not disciplined and brought under self-control, can allow all sorts of inappropriate thoughts. That's why Paul says, "Pray without ceasing" and let Christ take each thought captive.

Self-control of physical desires and needs is also a necessary discipline. We must be careful about what and how much we consume, what we love, and what we do. Again, Christ is our model and our strength. "Give us our daily bread" in the Lord's Prayer means give us only what we need and not everything we want.

We live in a culture out of control. "If it feels good, do it." We must swim against the stream to maintain our commitment to Christ.

What do you do to maintain self-control in your life? What are some of the temptations you struggle with, and what are the helps you use?

Read: Other Voices

Appendix

Any of these sheets can be photocopied and used in the teaching sessions. The first three are "bookmarks" which can be printed on cardstock, cut apart and given to the participants.

PRAYER RULE

ADORATION
Praise
Thanksgiving

CONFESSION
Admit wrongs
Ask forgiveness

PERSONAL NEEDS
Strength
Insight
Guidance
Comfort

INTERCESSION
Family
Friends
Enemies

SILENCE
Listening to God through
Centering Prayer

LOVE (AGAPE)
1 Cor. 13

SUFFERS LONG
DOES NOT ENVY
IS KIND
DOES NOT PARADE ITSELF
NOT PUFFED UP
DOES NOT BEHAVE RUDELY
DOES NOT SEEK ITS OWN
NOT PROVOKED
THINKS NO EVIL
DOES NOT REJOICE IN INIQUITY
REJOICES IN THE TRUTH
BEARS ALL THINGS
BELIEVES ALL THINGS
HOPES ALL THINGS
ENDURES ALL THINGS
LOVE NEVER FAILS

LOVE (AGAPE)
1 Cor. 13

SUFFERS LONG
DOES NOT ENVY
IS KIND
DOES NOT PARADE ITSELF
NOT PUFFED UP
DOES NOT BEHAVE RUDELY
DOES NOT SEEK ITS OWN
NOT PROVOKED
THINKS NO EVIL
DOES NOT REJOICE IN INIQUITY
REJOICES IN THE TRUTH
BEARS ALL THINGS
BELIEVES ALL THINGS
HOPES ALL THINGS
ENDURES ALL THINGS
LOVE NEVER FAILS

LOVE (AGAPE)
1 Cor. 13

SUFFERS LONG
DOES NOT ENVY
IS KIND
DOES NOT PARADE ITSELF
NOT PUFFED UP
DOES NOT BEHAVE RUDELY
DOES NOT SEEK ITS OWN
NOT PROVOKED
THINKS NO EVIL
DOES NOT REJOICE IN INIQUITY
REJOICES IN THE TRUTH
BEARS ALL THINGS
BELIEVES ALL THINGS
HOPES ALL THINGS
ENDURES ALL THINGS
LOVE NEVER FAILS

LOVE (AGAPE)
1 Cor. 13

SUFFERS LONG
DOES NOT ENVY
IS KIND
DOES NOT PARADE ITSELF
NOT PUFFED UP
DOES NOT BEHAVE RUDELY
DOES NOT SEEK ITS OWN
NOT PROVOKED
THINKS NO EVIL
DOES NOT REJOICE IN INIQUITY
REJOICES IN THE TRUTH
BEARS ALL THINGS
BELIEVES ALL THINGS
HOPES ALL THINGS
ENDURES ALL THINGS
LOVE NEVER FAILS

FRUITS OF THE SPIRIT	FRUITS OF THE SPIRIT	FRUITS OF THE SPIRIT
*****	*****	*****
LOVE	LOVE	LOVE
JOY	JOY	JOY
PEACE	PEACE	PEACE
PATIENCE	PATIENCE	PATIENCE
KINDNESS	KINDNESS	KINDNESS
GOODNESS	GOODNESS	GOODNESS
FAITHFULNESS	FAITHFULNESS	FAITHFULNESS
GENTLENESS	GENTLENESS	GENTLENESS
SELF-CONTROL	SELF-CONTROL	SELF-CONTROL
Gal. 5:22-23	Gal. 5:22-23	Gal. 5:22-23

How to Pray

PREPARE: Read a Psalm, either 23 or 91 or one of your choice.

PRAISE: Praise God for who He is and thank Him for all He has done for you. (I Thess. 5: 17)

REPENT: Ask God to forgive you for the wrongs you have done, ask Him to help you to forgive the ones who have wronged you, and, most importantly, FORGIVE YOURSELF! (Mark: 11 :25)

ASK: Make all your requests known to God, tell Him everything you need and are concerned about: your fears, your hopes, your doubts, everything. (Phil. 4:4-6)

INTERCEDE: Tell Him your concerns for others: family, friends, neighbors, fellow inmates. (I Tim. 2:1-2)

LORD'S PRAYER: Close your prayer time with the prayer Jesus taught His disciples to pray. (Matt. 6:9-13)

REMEMBER: God is your good Shepherd; He wants you to come to Him. If you are lost in any way, He is seeking you. He stands at the door and knocks, waiting for you to open so he can come in and "sup" (have fellowship) with you.

--Cut Apart To Distribute--

How to Pray

PREPARE: Read a Psalm, either 23 or 91 or one of your choice.

PRAISE: Praise God for who He is and thank Him for all He has done for you. (I Thess. 5: 17)

REPENT: Ask God to forgive you for the wrongs you have done, ask Him to help you to forgive the ones who have wronged you, and, most importantly, FORGIVE YOURSELF! (Mark: 11 :25)

ASK: Make all your requests known to God, tell Him everything you need and are concerned about: your fears, your hopes, your doubts, everything. (Phil. 4:4-6)

INTERCEDE: Tell Him your concerns for others: family, friends, neighbors, fellow inmates. (I Tim. 2:1-2)

LORD'S PRAYER: Close your prayer time with the prayer Jesus taught His disciples to pray. (Matt. 6:9-13)

REMEMBER: God is your good Shepherd; He wants you to come to Him. If you are lost in any way, He is seeking you. He stands at the door and knocks, waiting for you to open so he can come in and "sup" (have fellowship) with you.

Centering Prayer

Centering prayer is a way of being silent before God to deepen your relationship with Him and to gradually transform you into the Christlike person He wants you to become. It doesn't replace your other prayers, but only makes them more effective. It has been practiced from the earliest days of Christianity. This section is taken from Thomas Keating's book: "Open Mind, Open Heart."

Guidelines to Centering Prayer

1. Choose a word that you can hold onto as you move into God's presence. This word shows God that you desire to move more closely to Him. The word could be: Lord, Jesus, Love, Peace, Surrender, etc. Keep this word through your prayer time.

2. Sit comfortably with your eyes closed and begin to say that special word. This lets God know you are opening up to His presence.

3. When thoughts arise, which they will do, return gently to your special holy word. These thoughts could be memories, feelings, images, reflections, etc. They should be gently released by saying the word you have chosen.

4. The prayer period should last about 20 minutes. If possible, do it first thing in the morning and in the afternoon or early evening.

5. The principle effects of centering prayer are experienced in daily life, not in the period of centering prayer itself.

6. Bible study is essential to provide the basis for centering prayer, for you are opening up to becoming more Christlike, and Bible study tells us who Christ is.

7. A support group praying and sharing together once a week helps you stay with your prayer rule.

What Centering Prayer is Not:

1. It is not a technique.

2. It is not a relaxation exercise.

3. It is not a form of self-hypnosis

4. It is not a charismatic gift

5. It is not limited to "feeling" the presence of God.

What Centering Prayer is:

1. It is at the same time a relationship with God and a discipline to foster that relationship.

2. It is an exercise of faith, hope and love.

3. It is a movement beyond conversation with Christ to communion with Him.

4. It uses the language of God which is silence.

ST. PATRICK'S BREASTPLATE

Taken from: https://www.ourcatholicprayers.com/st-patricks-breastplate.html

St. Patrick's Breastplate is a popular prayer attributed to one of Ireland's most beloved patron saints. According to tradition, St. Patrick wrote it in 433 A.D. for divine protection before successfully converting the Irish King Leoghaire and his subjects from paganism to Christianity. (The term breastplate refers to a piece of armor worn in battle.)

More recent scholarship suggests its author was anonymous. In any case, this prayer certainly reflects the spirit with which St. Patrick brought our faith to Ireland! St. Patrick's Breastplate, also known as The Lorica of Saint Patrick was popular enough to inspire a hymn based on this text as well. (This prayer has also been called The Cry of the Deer.)

I arise today
Through a mighty strength, the invocation of the Trinity,
Through belief in the Threeness,
Through confession of the Oneness
of the Creator of creation.

I arise today
Through the strength of Christ's birth with His baptism,
Through the strength of His crucifixion with His burial,
Through the strength of His resurrection with His ascension,
Through the strength of His descent for the judgment of doom.

I arise today
Through the strength of the love of cherubim,
In the obedience of angels,
In the service of archangels,
In the hope of resurrection to meet with reward,
In the prayers of patriarchs,
In the predictions of prophets,
In the preaching of apostles,
In the faith of confessors,
In the innocence of holy virgins,
In the deeds of righteous men.

I arise today, through
The strength of heaven,
The light of the sun,
The radiance of the moon,
The splendor of fire,
The speed of lightning,

The swiftness of wind,
The depth of the sea,
The stability of the earth,
The firmness of rock.

I arise today, through
God's strength to pilot me,
God's might to uphold me,
God's wisdom to guide me,
God's eye to look before me,
God's ear to hear me,
God's word to speak for me,
God's hand to guard me,
God's shield to protect me,
God's host to save me
From snares of devils,
From temptation of vices,
From everyone who shall wish me ill,
afar and near.

I summon today
All these powers between me and those evils,
Against every cruel and merciless power
that may oppose my body and soul,
Against incantations of false prophets,
Against black laws of pagandom,
Against false laws of heretics,
Against craft of idolatry,
Against spells of witches and smiths and wizards,
Against every knowledge that corrupts man's body and soul;
Christ to shield me today
Against poison, against burning,
Against drowning, against wounding,
So that there may come to me an abundance of reward.

Christ with me,
Christ before me,
Christ behind me,
Christ in me,
Christ beneath me,
Christ above me,
Christ on my right,
Christ on my left,
Christ when I lie down,

Christ when I sit down,
Christ when I arise,
Christ in the heart of every man who thinks of me,
Christ in the mouth of everyone who speaks of me,
Christ in every eye that sees me,
Christ in every ear that hears me.

[Note that people sometimes pray a shorter version of this prayer just with these 15 lines about Christ above. The conclusion follows below.]

I arise today
Through a mighty strength, the invocation of the Trinity,
Through belief in the Threeness,
Through confession of the Oneness
of the Creator of creation.

The Serenity Prayer

God, grant me the serenity

to accept the things I cannot change,

the courage to change the things I can,

and the wisdom to know the difference.

Living one day at a time,

enjoying one moment at a time;

accepting hardship as a pathway to peace;

taking, as Jesus did,

this sinful world as it is,

not as I would have it;

trusting that You will make all things right

if I surrender to Your will;

so that I may be reasonable happy in this life

and supremely happy with You forever in the next.

Lenten Prayer of St. Ephrem

O Lord and Master of my life, take from me the spirit of sloth, despair, lust of power, and idle talk. But give rather the spirit of chastity, humility, patience, and love to Thy servant.

Yea, O Lord and King, grant me to see my own transgressions, and not to judge my brother, for blessed art Thou, unto ages of ages. Amen.

Prayer for the Beginning of the Day

O Lord, grant me to greet the coming day in peace, help me in all things to rely upon Your holy will. In every hour of the day reveal Your will to me. Bless my dealings with all who surround me. Teach me to treat all that comes to me throughout the day with peace of soul and with firm conviction that Your will governs all. In all my deeds and words, guide my thoughts and feelings. In unforseen events, let me not forget that all are sent by You. Teach me to act firmly and wisely, without embittering and embarrassing others. Give me strength to bear the fatigue of the coming day with all that it shall bring. Direct my will, teach me to pray. And, Yourself, pray in me. Amen

A Table of Psalms by Theme

God the Creator.	8, 19, 33, 65, 111, 104, 145, 147.
God the Redeemer.	15, 33, 102, 103, 111, 113, 114, 126, 130, 138.
God the Judge.	1, 7, 11, 46, 50, 62, 75, 76, 82, 90, 96, 97, 98.
God's Glory.	18, 29, 99, 36, 46, 148, 150.
God's Sovereignty.	24, 46, 47, 72, 89, 93, 96, 97, 98, 99, 112, 146, 145.
God's Wisdom.	33, 104, 111, 113, 139, 145, 147.
God's Law.	19, 50, 62, 111, 119, 147. 23, 33, 34, 37, 89, 121, 124, 139, 145, 146, 147.
God's Mercy.	23, 32, 57, 61, 62, 63, 73, 77, 85, 86, 100, 103, 118, 130, 145.
The Incarnation.	2, 8, 85, 89, 102, 110, 111, 113, 132.
The Passion.	22, 40, 42, 54, 69, 88, 116, 130.
The Church.	46, 48, 84, 111, 122, 133, 147.
Worship.	5, 26, 43, 63, 65, 66, 67, 84, 96, 100, 102, 116, 122, 138.
Thanksgiving.	30, 65, 67, 92, 98, 100, 111, 103, 107, 116, 134, 138, 145, 147, 148, 150.
Prayer.	4, 5, 17, 20, 28, 31, 54, 61, 84, 86, 102, 141, 142.
Trust in God.	27, 31, 57, 62, 63, 71, 73, 77, 91, 118, 121, 123, 124, 125, 143, 146.
God our Refuge.	4, 17, 20, 37, 46, 49, 54, 61, 71, 91, 103, 121, 146.
Divine Guidance.	25, 43, 80, 85, 111, 112.
In Time of Trouble.	3, 11, 12, 13, 18, 20, 30, 40, 46, 49, 57, 62, 63, 80, 85, 86, 90, 107, 118, 144, 146.
Righteousness.	1, 11, 12, 15, 18, 19, 26, 34, 40, 92, 111, 112.
Peace.	29, 46, 76, 85, 98, 100, 124, 125, 126.
The Transitoriness of Life.	39, 49, 90, 102.
The Hope of Immortality.	16, 30, 42, 49, 66, 73, 103, 116, 121, 139, 146.
Morning.	3, 5, 20, 63, 90, 143.
Evening.	4, 13, 16, 17, 31, 77, 91, 121, 134.
Penitential Psalms.	6, 32, 38, 51, 102, 130, 143.
Preparation for Holy Communion.	23, 25, 26, 36, 41, 43, 63, 84, 85, 86, 122, 130, 133, 139.
Thanksgiving after Holy Communion.	8, 15, 18, 19, 27, 29, 30, 34, 100, 103, 110, 118, 145, 150.

TIPS FOR A YOUNG PERSON ENTERING PRISON

1. Your body is in prison, but your mind and spirit are not unless you let them be. You can use this time to learn and enrich yourself or to stagnate and focus on negatives. You have a choice.

2. Committing a crime does not doom a person to committing other offenses or to an overwhelmingly painful or unproductive life. Recognize how your thinking or judgment went wrong and whether you were covering depression and anxiety with drugs or alcohol. This is the beginning of change.

3. Do not emotionally disconnect from people who care about you. Be honest about what is happening in prison. It is better to be honest so the people who care can realistically and emotionally support you.

4. Find opportunities for creativity and beauty in your life, whether it is writing and playing music, writing or reading poetry, or something as simple as appreciating the sunset. This will give you mental time out and protect your sanity.

5. Observe people and carefully decide who you want for allies or friends. Do not align yourself with the first strong person you meet or a person who does you a favor or gives you food. Some people befriend only to exploit.

6. You do not have to talk to other inmates about your crime unless you choose to.

7. Some inmates only feel good about themselves or feel they can justify their own misdeeds if they can bring others down to their level. Some like to antagonize and enrage others just for the thrill of seeing them angry or fighting.

8. Do not believe everything inmates tell you. Sometimes they like to scare you so they can feed on your fear. Check out anything you are concerned about with a staff member.

9. Do not worry if you feel you are different or do not "fit in." This may mean you need time to settle in or that you are not used to a criminal lifestyle or thinking like a criminal.

10. You can feel guilty because that is what helps us to learn from our mistakes. However, feeling shame about who we are is not helpful; it just keeps us in the same place. With guilt, you can change, let go, and begin to feel better, but shame puts you into "all or nothing" irrational thinking.

11. Develop your spiritual self. You are much more than body and mind. Find spiritual guidance—not the "hellfire, brimstone, and judgment" kind, but the kind that emphasizes grace, reconciliation, and your personal value as a child of God.

12. Do not allow other inmates or prison employees define who you are. Do not believe the negative labels that people may assign you; they do not know the real you.

13. Eat properly. Do not use caffeine or sweets to excess. A number of inmates with sleep problems use too much caffeine.

14. Try to maintain a regular sleep schedule. Many inmates with sleep disorders began by trying to sleep their time away. Consequently, they were not able to sleep, except for "cat naps." Exercise so you will be tired at bedtime. Stress intensifies and thinking becomes distorted if you do not sleep well.

15. Learn stress management, such as breathing exercises, Progressive Muscle Relaxation, meditation, guided imagery or visualization, exercise, writing in a journal, etc.

16. Constantly remind yourself that you only can control you and no one else. You cannot force anyone else to change his opinions or behavior. It is not your responsibility to "teach a lesson" to anyone.

17. Do not accept the convict code.

   a. It is not we (the inmates) against them (the officers). If you accept the "we vs. them" premise, you are open to other kinds of criminal thinking, violating the rules, and getting more time.
   b. Be honest and direct when questioned by the authorities, yet do not be a tattletale.
   c. Do not use violence to get even for wrongs you may experience. When you hurt someone else, you also hurt yourself emotionally
   d. Recognize who has the power/control in prison. The officers do have the authority to tell you what to do, and the staff members have the power to punish. You will rarely win in a difference with an officer, especially if you argue.
   e. Do not justify your actions by saying if you do not do something to a person first, he will do it to you.
   f. Do not take on the persona of the "tough guy" (talking or acting tough or "spoiling" for a fight.) If you get the reputation with officers as a troublemaker, they will watch you more closely and look for ways to "write you up." Besides, the label will stick with you even after you try to behave differently.
   g. Avoid gambling or getting into any kind of debt. You could be obligated to commit illegal activities for the one to whom you are indebted or find yourself in physical danger. A subscription to Christian daily devotions can be ordered, free of charge, to "Forward Day by Day" from Forward Movement, 412 Sycamore St. Cincinnati OH, 45202

* These "Tips" were compiled by Billie Stockton. She has given permission to have them reprinted here.

AMERICAN BIBLE ACADEMY
Pre-Enrollment Form

FREE BIBLE COURSE PRE-ENROLLMENT APPLICATION
SOLICITUD PRE-MATRICULA DE UN CURSO BÍBLICO GRATUITO

Please Print or Type and do not use abbreviations, and mark N/A if not applicable.
Por favor, letra de molde y no utilice abreviaturas, y marque N / A si no es aplicable.

Please provide the following contact information:
Por favor, provea la siguiente información para que podamos hacer contacto con Ud.

Name / Nombre: First [ ] Middle: [ ] Last: [ ]
Inmate # or ID# / # del encarcelado o # ID: [ ]
Facility / Instalación: [ ]
Location within Facility / Lugar dentro de la Instalación: [ ]
Address / Dirección postal: [ ]
City / Ciudad: [ ]
State / Estado: [ ]
Zip Code / Código postal: [ ]
Email: [ ]

I am an inmate requesting a free Bible Course in ENGLISH: [ ]
Soy un preso pidiendo cursos biblicos gratuitos en ESPAÑOL: [ ]

FREE COURSES ARE ONLY PROVIDED TO THE INCARCERATED AND LEGAL SPOUSE.
SE PROVEE CURSOS GRATUITOS SOLAMENTE PARA LOS ENCARCELADOS Y SUS CÓNYUGES LEGALES

ALL COURSES ARE PROFESSIONALLY TYPESET, PRINTED, AND BOUND INTO BEAUTIFUL 120 PAGE, SOFT COVER TEXTBOOKS!
¡TODOS LOS CURSOS SON PROFESIONALMENTE COMPUESTOS, IMPRESOS, Y ENCUADERNADOS CON TAPAS FLEXIBLES, RESULTANDO EN HERMOSOS LIBROS DE TEXTO DE 120 PÁGINAS!

Comments:
[ ]

Inmates may pre-enroll and request free courses by submitting this enrollment form or by writing to:

American Bible Academy
P.O. Box 1627
Joplin, Missouri 64802-1627

American Bible Academy will send additional enrollment information upon receiving this form.

ABOUT THE AUTHOR

Nancy Holloway, former college chaplain, has served in jail ministry for 16 years and currently represents St. Andrew Antiochian Orthodox Church in Lexington, KY. She has written articles on her work and is a member of the Prison Ministry Commission in Lexington, KY, which holds conferences addressing the needs of the incarcerated. You can reach her at nkholloway6@gmail.com.

Made in the USA
Las Vegas, NV
18 March 2023